Dart
Apprentice

First Edition

By Jonathan Sande & Matt Galloway

D1556168

Dart Apprentice

By Matt Galloway & Jonathan Sande

Copyright ©2020 Razeware LLC

ISBN: 978-1-950325-32-0

Dedications

"To the greatest coder of them all."

— *Jonathan Sande*

About the Authors

Jonathan Sande knows what it's like to bang his head against a wall because his app isn't working. He also understands the all-too-frequent feeling of still being completely lost even with twenty-seven browser tabs open. Once he finally does understand a topic, though, he enjoys writing the explanations and directions he wishes he had had when he started. Jonathan doesn't like wasting time rebuilding the same app on multiple platforms and in different programming languages, so that's why he uses Dart for mobile apps, Dart for desktop apps, Dart for the web and Dart on the server. You'd have a hard time convincing him to ever go back. Online he usually goes by the name Suragch, which is a Mongolian word meaning "student", a reminder to never stop learning. In his free time he also also enjoys studying human languages, reading about microbiology and discussing deep topics with open-minded people.

About the Editors

John Bennedict (JB) Lorenzo is the tech editor of this book. He is a mobile expert currently based in Berlin, but was born in the Philippines, where he began his career in tech. In his free time he does latin dancing, calisthenics, and traveling. He enjoys experiencing different cultures via food, language, stories, and travel.

Chris Belanger is an editor of this book. He is the former Editor-in-Chief of raywenderlich.com and now Chief Marketing Officer. In the programming world, Chris has over 25 years of experience with multiple database platforms, real-time industrial control systems, and enterprise healthcare information systems. When he kicks back, you can usually find Chris with guitar in hand, looking for the nearest beach, or exploring the lakes and rivers in his part of the world in a canoe.

About the Artist

Vicki Wenderlich is the designer and artist of the cover of this book. She is Ray's wife and business partner. She is a digital artist who creates illustrations, game art and a lot of other art or design work for the tutorials and books on raywenderlich.com. When she's not making art, she loves hiking, a good glass of wine and attempting to create the perfect cheese plate.

Acknowledgments

Acknowledgments are due to Matt Galloway, author of *Swift Apprentice*, upon which portions of this book are based.

Table of Contents

Book License 11

Before You Begin. **13**

What You Need 15

Book Source Code & Forums 17

About the Cover 19

Introduction 21
  Book sample projects 22
  How to read this book 22

Section I: Dart Apprentice **25**

Chapter 1: Hello, Dart!. 27
  Installing Visual Studio Code 29
  Installing the Dart SDK 29
  Dart on the command line 31
  Using VS Code for Dart development 35
  Key points. 40
  Where to go from here?. 40

Chapter 2: Expressions, Variables & Constants 41
  Commenting Code. 41
  Statements and expressions 44
  Arithmetic operations 45
  Naming data 49
  Increment and decrement 55
  Challenges 57
  Key points. 59
  Where to go from here?. 60

Chapter 3: Types & Operations 61
Data types in Dart 62
Strings 69
Working with strings in Dart.................................. 71
Object and dynamic types 81
Challenges 83
Key points... 85

Chapter 4: Control Flow 87
Making comparisons... 87
The if statement 94
Switch statements 98
Loops 104
Challenges... 112
Key points 114

Chapter 5: Functions 115
Function basics 116
Anonymous functions 128
Arrow functions 134
Challenges... 136
Key points 137
Where to go from here? 137

Chapter 6: Classes.. 139
Dart classes.. 140
Constructors 147
Dart objects 161
Static members.. 166
Challenges.. 170
Key points 171
Where to go from here? 172

Chapter 7: Nullability................................... 173

Null overview. 174
Handling nullable types 179
Challenges. 194
Key points 195
Where to go from here? 195

Chapter 8: Collections. 197
Lists. 197
Sets 206
Maps. 210
Higher order methods. 217
When to use lists, sets or maps 223
Challenges. 224
Key points 225
Where to go from here? 225

Chapter 9: Advanced Classes 227
Extending classes. 227
Abstract classes 236
Interfaces. 241
Mixins 248
Extension methods 251
Challenges. 257
Key points 258
Where to go from here? 258

Chapter 10: Asynchronous Programming. 261
Concurrency in Dart. 262
Futures 266
Streams. 278
Isolates 286
Challenges. 291
Key points 293

Where to go from here? 294

Conclusion... 295

Book License

By purchasing *Dart Apprentice*, you have the following license:

- You are allowed to use and/or modify the source code in *Dart Apprentice* in as many apps as you want, with no attribution required.

- You are allowed to use and/or modify all art, images and designs that are included in *Dart Apprentice* in as many apps as you want, but must include this attribution line somewhere inside your app: "Artwork/images/designs: from *Dart Apprentice*, available at www.raywenderlich.com".

- The source code included in *Dart Apprentice* is for your personal use only. You are NOT allowed to distribute or sell the source code in *Dart Apprentice* without prior authorization.

- This book is for your personal use only. You are NOT allowed to sell this book without prior authorization, or distribute it to friends, coworkers or students; they would need to purchase their own copies.

Before You Begin

This section tells you a few things you need to know before you get started, such as what you'll need for hardware and software, where to find the project files for this book, and more.

What You Need

To follow along with this book, you'll need the following:

- **Dart SDK**: A minimum version of 2.12.0 is required.

- **Visual Studio Code**: This book uses Visual Studio Code for all the examples. But you can use any other IDE if you prefer.

- **Dart Extension for VS Code**: To enable Dart in Visual Studio Code, you'll need to install the corresponding extension.

Book Source Code & Forums

Where to download the materials for this book

The materials for this book can be cloned or downloaded from the GitHub book materials repository:

- https://github.com/raywenderlich/da-materials/tree/editions/1.1

Forums

We've also set up an official forum for the book at forums.raywenderlich.com. This is a great place to ask questions about the book or to submit any errors you may find.

About the Cover

Dart Apprentice by Tutorials

Isn't the platypus an amazing animal? Think about it. The platypus is one of only two mammals that lay eggs rather than bear their offspring. They're practically blind and deaf, but are able to locate their prey through electroreception (like some dolphins!). They're also one of the few existing venomous mammals in the world.

When European naturalists first encountered them (they live in Australia, Tasmania and New Guinea) and examined a preserved platypus body in 1799, the naturalists thought the platypus was a hoax made up of several parts of different animals sewn together.

Come on, even its name, platypus, is cool!

So we couldn't think of a better animal to describe Dart. Dart is a client-optimized programming language for multi-platform apps. Just as platypuses are conformable on land or water, Dart can also adapt to completely different environments with ease.

And reminiscent of the platypus, Dart also looks like a combination of other things — in this case, programming languages. Dart was developed by Google as an object-oriented C-style syntax language and incorporates many of the best features of other modern programming languages. It can compile to either native code or Javascript and is the language used by Flutter to create native iOS, Android, Windows, Mac and Linux apps. How cool is that?

Exactly! As cool as a platypus!

Introduction

Dart is a general purpose programming language developed by Google. You can use it to develop web, server, desktop and mobile applications for iOS and Android. It's easy to learn (especially if you read this book) and also has great tooling support.

In many ways Dart is a boring language, and that's a good thing! It means that Dart is fast and easy to pick up. While Dart does have some unique characteristics, any knowledge you bring in from other object oriented or C-style languages will immediately be applicable. If you come here as a complete beginner to programming, Dart is a good place to start. The concepts that you'll learn in this book will give you a solid foundation in your coding career.

Don't let Dart's mundane syntax fool you. Dart is a modern and rapidly evolving language, and the things it allows you to do are both exciting and even historic in nature. Never before have you been able to create native applications for so many platforms using a single code base.

There's a good chance you picked up this book because of the Flutter UI framework. However, it was no accident that Flutter chose Dart as its language. The Dart virtual machine allows lightning fast development-time rebuilds, its JavaScript complier allows you to build for the web, and its ahead-of-time compiler creates fast native applications across mobile and desktop platforms and even for servers and embedded devices.

It's no wonder then that developers across the world have taken notice. The language has been climbing the charts for both fastest growing: https://octoverse.github.com/#top-languages and most loved https://bit.ly/2Q2ukO0. The wise developer takes note of industry trends and joins them.

So welcome to this book!

Book sample projects

Each chapter comes with supplemental material. In the chapter folder you'll find a folder called **starter** that contains a starter project with an empty `main` function. You can either open this empty project in your editor by going to **File ▸ Open** in the menu, or just create a new project in the way you'll learn in Chapter 1.

In addition to the starter project, chapters will also have a **final** folder, a **mini_exercise** folder and a **challenge** folder. You can refer to the **final** folder if you get lost during the lesson. It will contain the code from that lesson. Likewise, the **mini_exercise** and **challenge** folders will contain the answers to the mini-exercises and challenges in every chapter. You'll learn the most if you don't copy-and-paste this code but actually type it yourself.

Mini-exercises

You'll often find mini-exercises in middle of a chapter after learning about some topic. These are optional but generally easy to complete. Like the challenges, they'll help you solidify what you're learning.

Challenges

Challenges are an important part of *Dart Apprentice*. At the end of each chapter, the book will give you one or more tasks to accomplish that make use of the knowledge you learned in the chapter. Completing them will not only help you reenforce that knowledge but will also show that you've mastered it.

How to read this book

Each chapter of this book builds on the ones that precede it, so you'll find it easiest to understand if you progress through the chapters in order.

Dart Apprentice was written with the beginner in mind. If that's you, you'll learn the most by following along and trying each of the code examples, mini-exercises and challenges as you come to them. The way to learn to code is by writing code and experimenting with it. That can't be emphasized enough.

More advanced readers may want to skim the content of this book in order to get up and running quickly. If that's you, try the challenges at the end of every chapter. If they're easy, move on to the next chapter. If they're not, go back and read the relevant parts of the chapter and check the challenge solutions.

Finally, for all readers, raywenderlich.com is committed to providing quality, up-to-date learning materials. We'd love to have your feedback. What parts of the book gave you one of those aha learning moments? Was some topic confusing? Did you spot a typo or an error? Let us know at forums.raywenderlich.com and look for the particular forum category for this book. We'll make an effort to take your comments into account in the next update of the book.

Section I: Dart Apprentice

Begin your journey learning all the basic concepts you need to master this language. Follow along the easily and thoroughly explained concepts and you will be building Dart applications in a breeze.

Chapter 1: Hello, Dart!

This first chapter is designed to help you set up your development environment so that you can get the most out of the following chapters.

There are several different tools that Dart developers use when building apps:

- **DartPad**: This is a simple browser-based tool for writing and executing Dart code. It's available at dartpad.dev.

DartPad

- **IntelliJ IDEA**: IntelliJ is a powerful **Integrated Development Environment**, or **IDE**, that supports Dart development through a Dart plugin. Although Android Studio, a popular IDE for Flutter development, is built on IntelliJ, this book recommends that you use plain IntelliJ for pure Dart projects. The IntelliJ Dart plugin makes this an easier task than doing it in Android Studio.

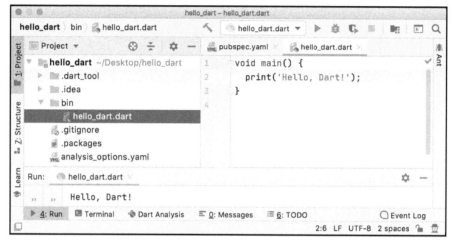

IntelliJ IDEA

- **Visual Studio Code**: Also known as **VS Code**, this is a lightweight IDE with a clean and simple interface. It fully supports Dart development with its Dart extension.

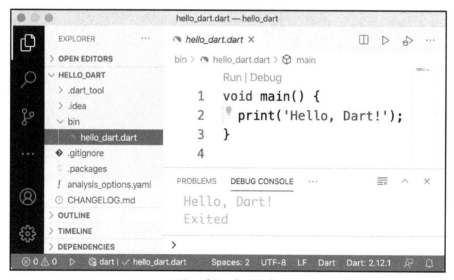

Visual Studio Code

This book uses Visual Studio Code for all of the examples contained within, but if you have another IDE you prefer, then by all means, continue using that one for your Dart development. If you don't have a preference, though, you'll find using VS Code an enjoyable experience. VS Code also supports Flutter development through an extension, so you won't be limiting yourself for future Flutter development if you choose to go the VS Code route now.

Installing Visual Studio Code

Visual Studio Code is a cross-platform, open-source IDE from Microsoft. It runs on Windows, MacOS and Linux, so unless the only device you've got at your disposal is a mobile phone, then you're covered!

> **Note**: If you *do* only have a mobile phone, don't despair! You can run the majority of the code examples in this book on dartpad.dev, which should work fine in any modern mobile browser.

Download Visual Studio Code at code.visualstudio.com, and follow the directions provided on the site to install it.

You'll also need the **Dart SDK**, which you'll install in the next section.

Installing the Dart SDK

The Dart **Software Development Kit**, or **SDK**, is a collection of command line tools that make it possible to develop Dart applications.

Go to https://dart.dev/get-dart and follow the directions on that site to download and install the Dart SDK on your platform.

> **Note**: Flutter comes with a copy of the Dart SDK, so if you've already installed a recent version of Flutter then you're good to go. At the time of this writing the current stable release of Flutter was 2.0, which includes Dart 2.12.

Verifying the Dart SDK installation

After you've installed Dart, run the following command in a terminal to ensure that it's working:

```
dart --version
```

You should see the current Dart version displayed, which at the time of this writing was **2.12.1**.

Contents of the SDK

Now check out what the Dart SDK offers you by entering the following command in the terminal:

```
dart help
```

You'll see a list of tools that make up the SDK. Although you won't directly interact with most of them in this book, it's helpful to know what they do:

- **analyze**: Your IDE uses this tool to tell you when you've made a mistake in your code. The sooner you know, the sooner you can fix it!

- **compile**: This tool compiles Dart code into an optimized native executable program for Windows, Linux or macOS. This is known as ahead-of-time, or **AOT**, compilation. Alongside native executables, web technologies are another major focus for Dart, so you can also use the compile tool to convert Dart code to JavaScript.

- **create**: This is for creating new Dart projects, which you'll do yourself in just a minute.

- **fix**: One of Dart's goals is to continue evolving as a language without becoming bloated by obsolete, or **deprecated**, code. The fix tool is there to help developers update their old projects to use the shiniest new Dart syntax.

- **format**: It's easy for the indentation in your code to get messed up. This nice little tool will automatically fix it for you.

- **migrate**: Version 2.12 was a major update to the Dart language with the addition of sound null safety, which you'll learn about in Chapter 7. This tool helps migrate old projects to use null safety. Since you're starting fresh, though, you won't need to migrate anything. Lucky you!

- **pub**: Pub is the name of the **package manager** for Dart, and pub is the tool that handles the job. A **package** is a collection of third-party code that you can use in your own Dart project. This can save you an incredible amount of time since you don't have to write that code yourself. You can browse the packages available to you on Pub by visiting pub.dev.

- **run**: This runs your Dart program in the Dart **Virtual Machine**, or **VM**. The Dart VM compiles your code right before it's needed. In contrast to AOT, this is known as just-in-time, or **JIT**, compilation, which will let you make small changes to your code and rerun it almost instantly. This is especially useful for applications like Flutter where you'll need to make lots of little changes as you refine the UI.

- **test**: Dart fully supports unit testing and this tool will help you get that done.

Dart on the command line

Now that you have the Dart SDK installed, you're going to use the Dart VM to run a few lines of code, first in a single file and then as a full project.

Running a single Dart file

Find or create a convenient folder on your computer where you can save the Dart projects that you create in this book. Create a new file in that folder and name it **hello.dart**.

Writing the code

Next add the following Dart code to that empty file:

```
void main() {
  print('Hello, Dart!');
}
```

This creates a Dart function named main. Inside that function, you call another function, print, which displays the text Hello, Dart! on the screen.

Running the code

Save the file, and then run the following command in the same folder as **hello.dart**:

```
dart run hello.dart
```

The run keyword is the run tool from the Dart SDK that you learned about earlier. It runs the code in **hello.dart** in the Dart VM.

You should now see the following output in the console:

```
Hello, Dart!
```

Congratulations! You've built and run your first Dart program.

Setting up a full Dart project

It's nice to be able to run a single file, but as you build bigger projects, you'll want to divide your code into manageable pieces and also include configuration and asset files. To do that you need to create a full Dart project. Remember that create tool? The time has come.

Creating the project

Go to the location where you want to create your project folder, and then run the following command in the terminal:

```
dart create hello_dart_project
```

This creates a simple Dart project with some default code.

Running the project

Enter the new folder you just created like so:

```
cd hello_dart_project
```

Now run the project with the following command:

```
dart run bin/hello_dart_project.dart
```

You'll see the text Hello world!, which is the output of the code in the default project that the create tool generated.

The run keyword is actually optional. Run the project again without it:

```
dart bin/hello_dart_project.dart
```

Again, Hello world! is the result.

The structure of a Dart project

Take a look at the structure and contents of the **hello_dart_project** folder:

The purposes of the main items in that folder are as follows:

- **bin**: Contains the executable Dart code.

- **hello_dart_project.dart**: Named the same as the project folder, the `create` tool generated this file for you to put your Dart code in.

- **.gitignore**: Formatted to exclude Dart-related files that you don't need if you're going to host your project on GitHub or another Git repository.

- **analysis_options.yaml**: Holds special rules that will help you detect issues with your code, a process known as **linting**.

- **CHANGELOG.md**: Holds a manually-curated Markdown-formatted list of the latest updates to your project. Whenever you release a new version of a Dart project, you should let other developers know what you've changed.

- **README.md**: Provides a basic (or not-so-basic) description of what your project does and how to use it. Other developers will appreciate this greatly.

- **pubspec.yaml**: Contains a list of the third-party Pub dependencies you want to use in your project. The name "pubspec" stands for "Pub specifications". You also set the version number of your project in this file.

> **Note**: **YAML** stands for "YAML Ain't Markup Language", one of those recursive acronyms that computer programmers like to amuse themselves with. YAML is a clean and readable way to format configuration files, and you'll come across this file type often in your Dart career.

Simple vs. full console app

When you created your project using the `create` tool above, it created a simple console app because that's the default. However, you can create other types of projects using the `--template` option.

For example, if you'd used the following command to create your project:

```
dart create --template console-full hello_dart_project
```

It would have given you the following directories and files:

There are two additional directories: **lib** and **test**. In larger projects, you'll have many **.dart** files that you'll organize under the **lib** folder. You'll also likely want to have tests to run against your Dart projects, and you can place those in the **test** folder.

For your work in this book, creating simple console projects will be enough. If you wish to create full console projects, though, it won't make a difference to your progress through this book.

Using VS Code for Dart development

You've created and run a project from the command line, but it's also possible to do the same thing from within VS Code. This section will walk you through that process.

Installing the Dart extension

Open Visual Studio Code, and on the left hand side you'll see a vertical toolbar called **Activity Bar**. Click the **Extensions icon**, which looks like four boxes. Then type **dart** in the search area. When the Dart extension appears, click the **Install button** to install it.

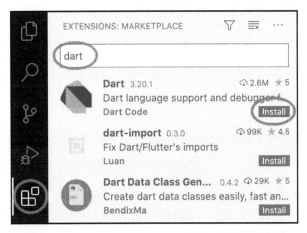

Now your VS Code installation supports Dart. Next you'll learn how to create a Dart project in VS Code.

Creating a new Dart project

The Dart extension in VS Code makes it easy to create a new Dart project. To see how this works, you'll recreate the same simple console project that you previously created from the command line.

To start, delete the **hello_dart_project** folder and its contents.

You can create a new project from the **Command Palette**. To access the Command Palette, either go to **View ▸ Command Palette...** in the menu, or press the shortcut **Command+Shift+P** on a Mac or **Control+Shift+P** on a PC.

Start typing **dart** to bring up a list of matching commands. Then choose **Dart: New Project**.

If you receive a message about Stagehand, then choose **Activate Stagehand**.

Next, choose **Simple Console Application** from the list.

As before, choose a location to save the project folder that VS Code will create, and name the project **hello_dart_project**.

Browsing the generated code

Open the file **hello_dart_project.dart** in the **bin** directory, and you'll see it contains the following code:

```dart
void main(List<String> arguments) {
  print('Hello world!');
}
```

The List<String> arguments portion is only necessary when creating command-line apps that take arguments. For example, take a look at the following imaginary terminal command that prints information about a country:

```
lookup -n spain
```

The command-line app name is lookup and the arguments are -n spain.

Since you won't be creating command-line apps in this book, you can remove the arguments portion to simplify things. Thus, replace the contents of **hello_dart_project.dart** with the following code:

```dart
void main() {
  print('Hello, Dart project!');
}
```

Running Dart in VS Code

To run your code, click the word **Run** that appears directly over the `main` function.

```
Run  Debug
void main() {
  print('Hello, Dart project!');
}
```

You'll see `Hello, Dart project!` appear in the debug console.

Exploring the VS Code UI

This is a good opportunity to explore the various parts of the Visual Studio Code user interface.

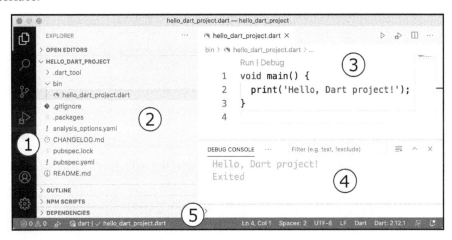

The numbers below correspond to the various areas of the user interface:

1. **Activity Bar**: Choose which content to show in the side bar.

2. **Side Bar**: The Explorer is displaying the current project and file.

3. **Editor**: Write your Dart code here.

4. **Panels**: Show program output, run terminal commands, and more.

5. **Status Bar**: Display information about the current project.

More ways to run your project

You ran your project earlier by pressing the **Run** label over the `main` function. Here are three more ways that you can run your project:

1. Choose **Run ▸ Start Debugging** from the menu.

2. Press **F5**.

3. Click the **triangular run button** in the top right corner.

All of these do the same thing. This time use **F5** to run the program, and you'll see `Hello, Dart project!` appear in the debug console again.

Project configuration file

Sometimes when pressing F5 to run your project, VS Code doesn't know where to look for the `main` function, and you'll see a message like this:

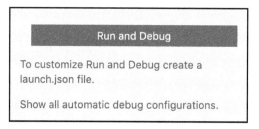

This is recommending that you create a **launch.json** file, which will help VS Code know which file to use to launch your app.

Since you originally ran your program by pressing the **Run** label, you may not have gotten this recommendation from VS Code. However, it's still a good idea to create a **launch.json** file, so you'll do that next.

Creating launch.json

Create the **launch.json** file by clicking the **Debug icon** in the **Activity Bar** and then clicking the link to **create a launch.json file** as shown in the image.

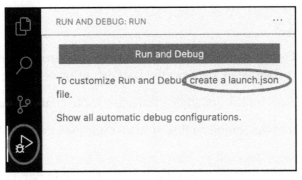

This will create a new **launch.json** file in the **.vscode** folder.

Updating the contents

Now replace the contents of **launch.json** with the following:

```
{
    "version": "0.2.0",
    "configurations": [
        {
            "name": "Dart",
            "type": "dart",
            "request": "launch",
            "program": "bin/hello_dart_project.dart"
        }
    ]
}
```

These are what the configuration elements mean:

- **name**: This is your project's configuration name. You can call it whatever you like.

- **type**: The type lets VS Code know that this is a Dart project.

- **request**: A request of launch tells VS Code that you want to run the project.

- **program**: This is the location where your program will start its execution. VS Code will look for the main function here so that it can launch your app.

Running your project again

Save your changes and run the file again by pressing **F5**. VS Code should be satisfied now that it knows where to look for the main function.

Excellent! You're all set to explore Dart further in the rest of this book.

Key points

- **Visual Studio Code** is an **Integrated Development Environment** that you can use to write Dart code when you have the Dart extension installed.

- The **Dart SDK** provides the underlying tools needed to compile and run Dart apps.

- Dart code run from the command line or in VS Code uses the **Dart Virtual Machine**.

- The VS Code window is divided into the **Activity Bar**, **Side Bar**, **Editor**, **Panel**, and **Status Bar**.

- **Pub** is the package manager that Dart uses to add third-party source code to your projects.

Where to go from here?

If you're new to Visual Studio Code, there's a lot more to learn about it. You can find many instructional resources by going to the **Help** menu.

Most of the time, you'll be writing Dart code using VS Code on a computer, but if you find yourself waiting in a long line at the supermarket, you can while away the time by writing Dart code at dartpad.dev, which will run on your mobile device. Try out the sample Dart and Flutter projects there.

Now that you have your programming environment all set up, you'll go on to start writing real Dart code in the next chapter. See you there!

Chapter 2: Expressions, Variables & Constants

By Jonathan Sande & Matt Galloway

Now that you've set up your Dart development environment, it's time to start writing some Dart code!

Follow along with the coding examples in this chapter. Simply create a project for your own use, and type in the code as you work through the examples.

Commenting Code

Dart, like most other programming languages, allows you to document your code through the use of comments. These allow you to write any text directly along side your code and are ignored by the compiler.

The depth and complexity of the code you write can obscure the big-picture details of why you wrote your code a certain way, or even what problem it is your code is solving. To prevent this, it's a good idea to document what you wrote so that the next human who passes through your code will be able to make sense of your work. That next human, after all, may be a future you!

The first way to write a comment in Dart is like so:

```
// This is a comment. It is not executed.
```

This is a single line comment.

You can stack up single line comments to allow you to write multi-line comments as shown below:

```
// This is also a comment,
// over multiple lines.
```

You may also create comment blocks by putting your comment text between /* and */:

```
/* This is also a comment. Over many...
many...
many lines. */
```

The start is denoted by /* and the end is denoted by */. Simple!

Dart also allows you to nest comments, like so:

```
/* This is a comment.
/* And inside it is
another comment. */
Back to the first. */
```

In addition to these two ways of writing comments, Dart also has a third type called **documentation comments**. Single-line documentation comments begin with ///, while block documentation comments are enclosed between /** and */. Here's an example of each:

```
/// I am a documentation comment
/// at your service.

/**
 * Me, too!
 */
```

Documentation comments are super useful because you can use them to generate...you guessed it...documentation! You'll want to add documentation comments to your code whenever you have a public API so that the users, and your future self, will know how your API works. Although this book won't go into depth on this, documentation comments even support **Markdown** formatting so that you can add elements like code examples or links to your comments.

> **Note**: To put it simply, an **API**, or **application programming interface**, is code that you share with other people or programs. You'll learn how to make your own API in Chapter 9.

The Flutter and Dart documentation is well-known for its detailed comments. And since the code for Flutter and Dart is open source, simply browsing through it is an excellent way to learn how great documentation comments are written.

In fact, you can try browsing that documentation right now. Take the Hello Dart program from Chapter 1:

```
void main() {
  print('Hello, Dart!');
}
```

In VS Code, **Command+Click** on a Mac, or **Control+Click** on a PC, the `print` keyword. VS Code will take you to the source code for that keyword and you'll see the documentation comments for `print`:

```
/// Prints a string representation of the object to the console.
void print(Object? object) {
```

Speaking of `print`, that's another useful tool when writing Dart code.

Printing output

`print` will output whatever you want to the debug console.

For example, consider the following code:

```
print('Hello, Dart Apprentice reader!');
```

Run this code and it'll output a nice message to the debug console, like so:

```
PROBLEMS    OUTPUT    DEBUG CONSOLE    TERMINAL
Hello, Dart Apprentice reader!
Exited
```

Adding `print` statements into your code is an easy way to monitor what's happening at a particular point in your code. Later, when you're ready to take your debugging to the next level, you can check out some of the more detailed logging packages on pub.dev.

You can print any expression in Dart. To learn what an expression is, though, keep reading.

Statements and expressions

Two important words that you'll often hear thrown about in programming language documentation are **statement** and **expression**. It's helpful to understand the difference between the two.

Statements

A **statement** is a command, something you tell the computer to do. In Dart, all simple statements end with a semicolon. You've already seen that with the `print` statement:

```
print('Hello, Dart Apprentice reader!');
```

The semicolon on the right finishes the statement.

People coming from languages that don't require semicolons may think they're unnecessary. However, due to Dart's special syntax and features, semicolons give the compiler the context it needs to properly understand the code.

In addition to simple statements, Dart also has **complex statements** and code blocks that use curly braces, but there's no need to add semicolons after the braces.

One example of a complex statement is the `if` statement:

```
if (someCondition) {
  // code block
}
```

No semicolons are needed on the lines with the opening or closing curly braces. You'll learn more about `if` statements and other control flow statements in Chapter 4.

Expressions

Unlike a statement, an **expression** doesn't *do* something; it *is* something. That is, an expression is a value, or is something that can be calculated as a value.

Here are a few examples of expressions in Dart:

```
42
3 + 2
'Hello, Dart Apprentice reader!'
x
```

The values can be numbers, text, or some other type. They can even be variables such as x whose value isn't known until runtime.

Coming up next, you'll see many more examples of expressions.

Arithmetic operations

In this section, you'll learn about the various **arithmetic operations** that Dart has to offer by seeing how they apply to numbers. In later chapters, you'll learn about operations for types beyond simple numbers.

Simple operations

Each operation in Dart uses a symbol known as the **operator** to denote the type of operation it performs. Consider the four arithmetic operations you learned in your early school days: addition, subtraction, multiplication and division. For these simple operations, Dart uses the following operators:

- Add: +

- Subtract: −

- Multiply: *

- Divide: /

These operators are used like so:

```
2 + 6
10 - 2
2 * 4
24 / 3
```

Each of these lines is an expression, because each can be calculated down to a value. In these cases, all four expressions have the same value: 8. Notice how the code looks similar to how you would write the operations out with pen and paper.

Check the answers yourself in VS Code using a print statement:

```
print(2 + 6);
```

Dart ignores whitespace, so you can remove the spaces surrounding the operator:

```
2+6
```

However, it's often easier to read expressions when you have white space on either side. In fact, the **dart format** tool in the Dart SDK will format your code according to the standard whitespace formatting rules. In VS Code, you can apply `dart format` with the keyboard shortcut **Shift+Option+F** on a Mac or **Shift+Alt+F** on a PC.

> **Note**: This book won't always explicitly tell you to `print(X)`, where X is some Dart expression that you're learning about, but you should proactively do this yourself to check the value.

Decimal numbers

All of the operations above use whole numbers, more formally known as **integers**. However, as you know, not every number is whole.

For example, consider the following:

```
22 / 7
```

If you're used to another language that uses integer division by default, you might expect the result to be 3. However, Dart gives you the standard decimal answer:

```
3.142857142857143
```

If you actually did want to perform integer division, then you could use the ~/ operator:

```
22 ~/ 7
```

This produces a result of 3.

The ~/ operator is officially called the **truncating division operator** when applied to numbers. If you squint, the tilde kind of looks like an elephant trunk, so that might help you remember what it does. Or not.

The Euclidean modulo operation

Dart also has more complex operations you can use. All of them are standard mathematical operations, just not as common as the others. You'll take a look at them now.

The first of these is the **Euclidean modulo operation**. That's a complex name for an easy task. In division, the denominator goes into the numerator a whole number of times, plus a remainder. This remainder is what the Euclidean modulo operation calculates. For example, 10 modulo 3 equals 1, because 3 goes into 10 three times, with a remainder of 1.

In Dart, the Euclidean modulo operator is the % symbol. You use it like so:

```
28 % 10
```

In this case, the result equals 8, because 10 goes into 28 twice with a remainder of 8.

Order of operations

Of course, it's likely that when you calculate a value, you'll want to use multiple operators. Here's an example of how to do this in Dart:

```
((8000 / (5 * 10)) - 32) ~/ (29 % 5)
```

Note the use of parentheses, which in Dart serve two purposes: to make it clear to anyone reading the code — including yourself — what you meant, and to disambiguate the intended order of operations. For example, consider the following:

```
350 / 5 + 2
```

Does this equal 72 (350 divided by 5, plus 2) or 50 (350 divided by 7)? Those of you who paid attention in school will be screaming, "72"! And you'd be right.

Dart uses the same reasoning and achieves this through what's known as **operator precedence**. The division operator (/) has a higher precedence than the addition operator (+), so in this example, the code executes the division operation first.

If you wanted Dart to perform the addition first — that is, so the expression will return 50 instead of 72 — then you could use parentheses, like so:

```
350 / (5 + 2)
```

The precedence rules are the same as you learned in school. Multiplication and division have equal precedence. Addition and subtraction are equal in precedence to each other, but are lower in precedence than multiplication and division.

The ~/ and % operators have the same precedence as multiplication and division. If you're ever uncertain about what precedence an operator has, you can always use parentheses to be sure the expression evaluates as you want it to.

Math functions

Dart also has a large range of math functions. You never know when you'll need to flex those trigonometry muscles, especially when you're a pro at Dart and writing complex animations!

To use these math functions, add the following import to the top of your file:

```
import 'dart:math';
```

dart:math is one of Dart's core libraries. Adding the import statement tells the compiler that you want to use something from that library.

Now you can write the following:

```
sin(45 * pi / 180)
// 0.7071067811865475

cos(135 * pi / 180)
// -0.7071067811865475
```

These convert an angle from degrees to radians, and then compute the sine and cosine respectively. Notice how both make use of pi, which is a constant Dart provides you. Nice!

> **Note**: Remember that if you want to see the values of these mathematical expressions, you need to put them inside a print statement like this:
>
> ```
> print(sin(45 * pi / 180));
> ```

Then there's this:

```
sqrt(2)
// 1.4142135623730951
```

This computes the square root of 2.

Not mentioning these would be a shame:

```
max(5, 10)
// 10

min(-5, -10)
// -10
```

These compute the maximum and minimum of two numbers respectively.

If you're particularly adventurous you can even combine these functions like so:

```
max(sqrt(2), pi / 2)
// 1.5707963267948966
```

Mini-exercise

In the example above you found the sine of 45° by first converting 45° to radians and then using the Dart sin function, which works in radians, to calculate the result. Now print the value of 1 over the square root of 2 in Dart. Confirm that it equals the sine of 45°.

This is your first mini-exercise. You can find the answers in the **mini_exercise** folder in the supplemental materials that come with this book.

Naming data

At its simplest, computer programming is all about manipulating data, since everything you see on your screen can be reduced to numbers. Sometimes you represent and work with data as various types of numbers, but other times, the data comes in more complex forms such as text, images and collections.

In your Dart code, you can give each piece of data a name you can use to refer to that piece of data later. The name carries with it an associated **type** that denotes what sort of data the name refers to, such as text, numbers, or a date. You'll learn about some of the basic types in this chapter, and you'll encounter many other types throughout this book.

Variables

Take a look at the following:

```
int number = 10;
```

This statement declares a variable called number of type int. It then sets the value of the variable to the number 10. The int part of the statement is known as a **type annotation**, which tells Dart explicitly what the type is.

> **Note**: Thinking back to operators, here's another one. The equals sign, =, is known as the **assignment operator** because it assigns a value to a variable. This is different than the equals sign you are familiar with from math. That equals sign is more like the == **equality operator** in Dart, which you will learn about in Chapter 4.

If you want to change the value of a variable, then you can just give it a different value of the same type:

```
int number = 10;
number = 15;
```

The type `int` can store integers. The way you store decimal numbers is like so:

```
double apple = 3.14159;
```

This is similar to the `int` example. This time, though, the variable is a `double`, a type that can store decimals with high precision.

For readers who are familiar with object-oriented programming, you'll be interested to learn that `10`, `3.14159` and every other value that you can assign to a variable are objects in Dart. In fact, Dart doesn't have the primitive variable types that exist in some languages. Everything is an object. Although `int` and `double` look like primitives, they're subclasses of `num`, which is a subclass of `Object`.

With numbers as objects, this lets you do some interesting things:

```
10.isEven
// true

3.14159.round()
// 3
```

> **Note**: Don't worry if you're not familiar with object-oriented programming. You'll learn all about it in Chapters 6 and 9.

Type safety

Dart is a type-safe language. That means once you tell Dart what a variable's type is, you can't change it later. Here's an example:

```
int myInteger = 10;
myInteger = 3.14159; // No, no, no. That's not allowed.
```

3.14159 is a double, but you already defined myInteger as an int. No changes allowed!

Dart's type safety will save you countless hours when coding, since the compiler will tell you immediately whenever you try to give a variable the wrong type. This prevents you from having to chase down bugs after you experience runtime crashes.

Of course, sometimes it's useful to be able to assign related types to the same variable. That's still possible. For example, you could solve the problem above, where you want myNumber to store both an integer and floating-point value, like so:

```
num myNumber;
myNumber = 10;      // OK
myNumber = 3.14159; // OK
myNumber = 'ten';   // No, no, no.
```

The num type can be either an int or a double, so the first two assignments work. However, the string value 'ten' is of a different type, so the compiler complains.

Now, if you like living dangerously, you can throw safety to the wind and use the dynamic type. This lets you assign any data type you like to your variable, and the compiler won't warn you about *anything*.

```
dynamic myVariable;
myVariable = 10;      // OK
myVariable = 3.14159; // OK
myVariable = 'ten';   // OK
```

But, honestly, don't do that. Friends don't let friends use dynamic. Your life is too valuable for that.

In Chapter 3 you'll learn more about types.

Type inference

Dart is smart in a lot of ways. You don't even have to tell it the type of a variable, and Dart can still figure out what you mean. The var keyword says to Dart, "Use whatever type is appropriate."

```
var someNumber = 10;
```

There's no need to tell Dart that 10 is an integer. Dart **infers the type** and makes someNumber an int. Type safety still applies, though:

```
var someNumber = 10;
someNumber = 15;      // OK
someNumber = 3.14159; // No, no, no.
```

Trying to set someNumber to a double will result in an error. Your program won't even compile. Quick catch; time saved. Thanks, Dart!

Constants

Dart has two different types of "variables" whose values never change. They are declared with the const and final keywords, and the following sections will show the difference between the two.

const constants

Variables whose value you can change are known as **mutable data**. Mutables certainly have their place in programs, but can also present problems. It's easy to lose track of all the places in your code that can change the value of a particular variable. For that reason, you should use **constants** rather than variables whenever possible. These unchangeable variables are known as **immutable data**.

To create a constant in Dart, use the const keyword:

```
const myConstant = 10;
```

Just as with var, Dart uses type inference to determine that myConstant is an int.

Once you've declared a constant, you can't change its data. For example, consider the following example:

```
const myConstant = 10;
myConstant = 0; // Not allowed.
```

This code produces an error:

```
Constant variables can't be assigned a value.
```

In VS Code, you would see the error represented this way:

```
int myConstant
Constant variables can't be assigned a value.
Try removing the assignment, or remove the modifier 'const' from
the variable. dart(assignment_to_const)
Peek Problem (⌥F8)   No quick fixes available
myConstant = 0;
```

If you think "constant variable" sounds a little oxymoronic, just remember that it's in good company: virtual reality, advanced BASIC, readable Perl and internet security.

final constants

Often, you know you'll want a constant in your program, but you don't know what its value is at compile time. You'll only know the value after the program starts running. This kind of constant is known as a **runtime constant**.

In Dart const is only used for **compile-time constants**; that is, for values that can be determined by the compiler before the program ever starts running.

If you can't create a const variable because you don't know its value at compile time, then you must use the final keyword to make it a runtime constant. There are many reasons you might not know a value until after your program is running. For example, you might need to fetch a value from the server, or query the device settings, or ask a user to input their age.

Here is another example of a runtime value:

```
final hoursSinceMidnight = DateTime.now().hour;
```

DateTime.now() is a Dart function that tells you the current date and time when the code is run. Adding hour to that tells you the number of hours that have passed since the beginning of the day. Since that code will produce a different results depending on the time of day, this is most definitely a runtime value. So to make hoursSinceMidnight a constant, you must use the final keyword instead of const.

If you try to change the final constant after it's already been set:

```
hoursSinceMidnight = 0;
```

This will produce the following error:

```
The final variable 'hoursSinceMidnight' can only be set once.
```

You don't actually need to worry too much about the difference between `const` and `final` constants. As a general rule, try `const` first, and if the compiler complains, then make it `final`. The benefit of using `const` is it gives the compiler the freedom to make internal optimizations to the code before compiling it.

No matter what kind of variable you have, though, you should give special consideration to what you *call* it.

Using meaningful names

Always try to choose meaningful names for your variables and constants. Good names act as documentation and make your code easy to read.

A good name specifically describes the role of a variable or constant. Here are some examples of good names:

- `personAge`
- `numberOfPeople`
- `gradePointAverage`

Often a bad name is simply not descriptive enough. Here are some examples of bad names:

- `a`
- `temp`
- `average`

The key is to ensure that you'll understand what the variable or constant refers to when you read it again later. Don't make the mistake of thinking you have an infallible memory! It's common in computer programming to look back at your own code as early as a day or two later and have forgotten what it does. Make it easier for yourself by giving your variables and constants intuitive, precise names.

Also, note how the names above are written. In Dart, it's standard to use `lowerCamelCase` for variable and constant names. Follow these rules to properly case your names:

- Start with a lowercase letter.

- If the name is made up of multiple words, join them together and start every word after the first one with an uppercase letter.

- Treat abbreviations like words (for example, `sourceUrl` and `urlDescription`).

Mini-exercises

If you haven't been following along with these exercises in VS Code, now's the time to create a new project and try some exercises to test yourself!

1. Declare a constant of type `int` called `myAge` and set it to your age.

2. Declare a variable of type `double` called `averageAge`. Initially, set the variable to your own age. Then, set it to the average of your age and your best friend's age.

3. Create a constant called `testNumber` and initialize it with whatever integer you'd like. Next, create another constant called `evenOdd` and set it equal to `testNumber` modulo 2. Now change `testNumber` to various numbers. What do you notice about `evenOdd`?

Increment and decrement

A common operation that you'll need is to be able to **increment** or **decrement** a variable. In Dart, this is achieved like so:

```
var counter = 0;

counter += 1;
// counter = 1;

counter -= 1;
// counter = 0;
```

The counter variable begins as 0. The increment sets its value to 1, and then the decrement sets its value back to 0.

The += and -= operators are similar to the assignment operator (=), except they also perform an addition or subtraction. They take the current value of the variable, add or subtract the given value, and assign the result back to the variable.

In other words, the code above is shorthand for the following:

```
var counter = 0;
counter = counter + 1;
counter = counter - 1;
```

If you only need to increment or decrement by 1, then you can use the ++ or --
operators:

```
var counter = 0;
counter++; // 1
counter--; // 0
```

The *= and /= operators perform similar operations for multiplication and division,
respectively:

```
double myValue = 10;

myValue *= 3;   // same as myValue = myValue * 3;
// myValue = 30.0;

myValue /= 2;   // same as myValue = myValue / 2;
// myValue = 15.0;
```

Division in Dart produces a result with a type of double, so myValue could not be an
int.

Challenges

Before moving on, here are some challenges to test your knowledge of variables and constants. It's best if you try to solve them yourself, but solutions are available with the supplementary materials for this book if you get stuck.

Challenge 1: Variables

Declare a constant int called myAge and set it equal to your age. Also declare an int variable called dogs and set that equal to the number of dogs you own. Then imagine you bought a new puppy and increment the dogs variable by one.

Challenge 2: Make it compile

Given the following code:

```
age = 16;
print(age);
age = 30;
print(age);
```

Modify the first line so that the code compiles. Did you use var, int, final or const?

Challenge 3: Compute the answer

Consider the following code:

```
const x = 46;
const y = 10;
```

Work out what each answer equals when you add the following lines of code to the code above:

```
const answer1 = (x * 100) + y;
const answer2 = (x * 100) + (y * 100);
const answer3 = (x * 100) + (y / 10);
```

Challenge 4: Average rating

Declare three constants called rating1, rating2 and rating3 of type double and assign each a value. Calculate the average of the three and store the result in a constant named averageRating.

Challenge 5: Quadratic equations

A quadratic equation is something of the form

```
a·x² + b·x + c = 0.
```

The values of x which satisfy this can be solved by using the equation

```
x = (−b ± sqrt(b² − 4·a·c)) / (2·a).
```

Declare three constants named a, b and c of type `double`. Then calculate the two values for x using the equation above (noting that the ± means plus or minus, so one value of x for each). Store the results in constants called `root1` and `root2` of type double.

Key points

- Code comments are denoted by a line starting with //, or by multiple lines bookended with /* and */.

- Documentation comments are denoted by a line starting with /// or multiple lines bookended with /** and */.

- You can use print to write to the debug console.

- The arithmetic operators are:

```
Addition: +
Subtraction: -
Multiplication: *
Division: /
Truncating division: ~/
Modulo (remainder): %
```

- Dart has many functions including min, max, sqrt, sin and cos. You'll learn many more throughout this book.

- Constants and variables give names to data.

- Once you've declared a constant, you can't change its data, but you can change a variable's data at any time.

- If a variable's type can be inferred, you can replace the type with the var keyword.

- The const keyword is used for compile-time constants while final is used for runtime constants.

- Always give variables and constants meaningful names to save yourself and your colleagues headaches later.

- Operators that perform arithmetic, and then assign back to the variable, are:

```
Add and assign: +=
Subtract and assign: -=
Multiply and assign: *=
Divide and assign: /=
Increment by 1: ++
Decrement by 1: --
```

Where to go from here?

In this chapter, you learned about documentation comments and that you can use markdown formatting within them. If you aren't familiar with Markdown, it would be well worth your time to learn it. Dart supports CommonMark, so commonmark.org is a good place to start learning.

Speaking of documentation, it's also worth your while to develop the habit of reading source code. Read it like you would a book, whether it's the Dart and Flutter source code, or a third-party library. This will often teach you much more than you can learn from other sources.

In the next chapter, you'll dive even deeper into Dart's type system and the operations that you can perform on them, especially the `String` type. See you there!

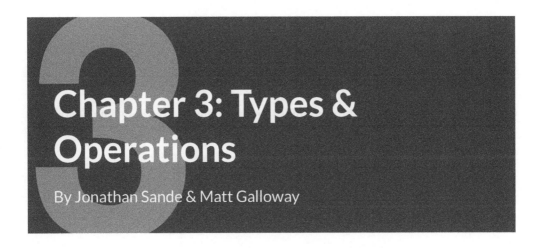

Chapter 3: Types & Operations

By Jonathan Sande & Matt Galloway

Life is full of variety, and that variety expresses itself in different types. What type of toothpaste do you use? Spearmint? Cinnamon? What's your blood type? A? B? O+? What type of ice cream do you like? Vanilla? Strawberry? Praline pecan fudge swirl? Having names for all of these different things helps you talk intelligently about them. It also helps you to recognize when something is out of place. After all, no one brushes their teeth with praline pecan fudge swirl. Though it does sound kind of nice.

Programming types are just as useful as real life types. They help you to categorize all the different kinds of data you use in your code.

In Chapter 2, you learned how to name data using variables and also got a brief introduction to Dart data types. In this chapter, you'll learn even more about types and what you can do with them. There will be a particular focus on strings, which are used to represent text.

Data types in Dart

In Dart, a **type** is a way to tell the compiler how you plan to use some data. By this point in this book, you've already seen the following types:

- `int`
- `double`
- `num`
- `dynamic`
- `String`

The last one in that list, `String`, is the type used for text like `'Hello, Dart!'`.

Just as you don't brush your teeth with ice cream, Dart types keep you from trying to do silly things like dividing text or removing whitespace from a number.

Dart has even more built-in types than just the ones listed above. The basic ones, such as `int`, `double`, and `num` will serve you adequately in a great variety of programming scenarios, but when working on projects with specific needs, it'll be convenient to create custom types instead. A weather app, for example, may need a `Weather` type, while a social media app may need a `User` type. You'll learn how to create your own types in Chapter 4 and Chapter 6.

As you learned in Chapter 2, the root of all types is the `Object` type. This type defines a few core operations, such as testing for equality and describing the object in text. Every other type in Dart is a subtype of `Object`, and as a subtype, shares `Object`'s basic functionality.

Type inference

In the previous chapter, you also got a sneak peak at type inference in Dart, but you'll take some time to look at it in a little more depth now.

Annotating variables explicitly

It's fine to always explicitly add the **type annotation** when you declare a variable. This means writing the data type before the variable name.

```
int myInteger = 10;
double myDouble = 3.14;
```

You annotated the first variable with `int` and the second with `double`.

Creating constant variables

Declaring variables the way you did above makes them mutable. If you want to make them immutable, but still keep the type annotation, you can add `const` or `final` in front.

These forms of declaration are fine with `const`:

```
const int myInteger = 10;
const double myDouble = 3.14;
```

They're also fine with `final`:

```
final int myInteger = 10;
final double myDouble = 3.14;
```

> **Note**: Mutable data is convenient to work with because you can change it any time you like. However, many experienced software engineers have come to appreciate the benefits of immutable data. When a value is immutable, that means you can trust that no one will change that value after you create it. Limiting your data in this way prevents many hard-to-find bugs from creeping in, and also makes the program easier to reason about and to test.

Letting the compiler infer the type

While it's permissible to include the type annotation as in the example above, it's redundant. You're smart enough to know that `10` is an `int` and `3.14` is a `double`, and it turns out the Dart compiler can deduce this as well. The compiler doesn't need you to explicitly tell it the type every time — it can figure the type out on its own through a process called **type inference**. Not all programming languages have type inference, but Dart does — and it's a key component behind Dart's power as a language.

You can simply drop the type in most instances. For example, here are the constants from above without the type annotations:

```
const myInteger = 10;
const myDouble = 3.14;
```

In the absence of type annotation, Dart figures out the correct type for each constant above.

Checking the inferred type in VS Code

Sometimes, it can be useful to check the inferred type of a variable or constant. You can do this in VS Code by hovering your mouse pointer over the variable name. VS Code will display a popover like this:

```
    int myInteger
const myInteger = 10;
```

VS Code shows you the inferred type. In this example, the type is `int`.

It works for other types, too. Hovering your mouse pointer over `myDouble` shows that it's a `double`:

```
    double myDouble
const myDouble = 3.14;
```

Type inference isn't magic; Dart is simply doing what your own brain does very easily. Programming languages that don't use type inference often feel verbose, because you need to specify the (usually) obvious type each time you declare a variable or constant.

> **Note:** There are times when you'll want (or need) to explicitly include the type, either because Dart doesn't have enough information to figure it out, or because you want your intent to be clear to the reader. However, you'll see type inference used for most of the code examples in this book.

Checking the type at runtime

Your code can't hover a mouse pointer over a variable to check the type, but Dart does have a programmatic way of doing the same thing: the `is` keyword.

```
num myNumber = 3.14;
print(myNumber is double);
print(myNumber is int);
```

Run this to see the following result:

```
true
false
```

Recall that both `double` and `int` are subtypes of `num`. That means `myNumber` could store either type. In this case, `3.14` is a `double`, and not an `int`, which is what the `is` keyword checks for and confirms by returning `true` and `false` respectively. You'll learn more about the type for `true` and `false` values in Chapter 4.

Another option to see the type at runtime is to use the `runtimeType` property that is available to all types.

```
print(myNumber.runtimeType);
```

This prints `double` as expected.

Type conversion

Sometimes, you'll have data in one type, but need to convert it to another. The naïve way to attempt this would be like so:

```
var integer = 100;
var decimal = 12.5;
integer = decimal;
```

Dart will complain if you try to do that:

```
A value of type 'double' can't be assigned to a variable of type
'int'.
```

Some programming languages aren't as strict and will perform conversions like this silently. Experience shows this kind of silent, implicit conversion is a frequent source of software bugs and often hurts code performance. Dart disallows you from assigning a value of one type to another and avoids these issues.

Remember, computers rely on programmers to tell them what to do. In Dart, that includes being explicit about type conversions. If you want the conversion to happen, you have to say so!

Instead of simply assigning and hoping for implicit conversion, you need to explicitly say that you want Dart to convert the type. You can convert this `double` to an `int` like so:

```
integer = decimal.toInt();
```

The assignment now tells Dart, unequivocally, that you want to convert from the original type, `double`, to the new type, `int`.

> **Note**: In this case, assigning the decimal value to the integer results in a loss of precision: The integer variable ends up with the value 12 instead of 12.5. This is why it's important to be explicit. Dart wants to make sure you know what you're doing and that you may end up losing data by performing the type conversion.

Operators with mixed types

So far, you've only seen operators acting independently on integers or doubles. But what if you have an integer that you want to multiply with a double?

Take this example:

```
const hourlyRate = 19.5;
const hoursWorked = 10;
const totalCost = hourlyRate * hoursWorked;
```

hourlyRate is a double and hoursWorked is an int. What will the type of totalCost be? It turns out that Dart will make totalCost a double. This is the safest choice, since making it an int could cause a loss of precision.

If you actually do want an int as the result, then you need to perform the conversion explicitly:

```
const totalCost = (hourlyRate * hoursWorked).toInt();
```

The parentheses tell Dart to do the multiplication first, and after that, to take the result and convert it to an integer value. However, the compiler complains about this:

```
Const variables must be initialized with a constant value.
```

The problem is that toInt is a runtime method. This means that totalCost can't be determined at compile time, so making it const isn't valid. No problem; there's an easy fix. Just change const to final:

```
final totalCost = (hourlyRate * hoursWorked).toInt();
```

Now totalCost is an int.

Ensuring a certain type

Sometimes you want to define a constant or variable and ensure it remains a certain type, even though what you're assigning to it is of a different type. You saw earlier how you can convert from one type to another. For example, consider the following:

```
const wantADouble = 3;
```

Here, Dart infers the type of `wantADouble` as `int`. But what if you wanted the constant to store a `double` instead?

One thing you could do is the following:

```
final actuallyDouble = 3.toDouble();
```

This uses type conversion to convert 3 into a `double` before assignment, as you saw earlier in this chapter.

Another option would be to not use type inference at all, and to add the `double` annotation:

```
const double actuallyDouble = 3;
```

The number 3 is an integer, but literal number values that contain a decimal point cannot be integers, which means you could have avoided this entire discussion had you started with:

```
const wantADouble = 3.0;
```

Sorry! :]

Casting down

At other times, you may have a variable of some general supertype, but you need functionality that is only available in a subtype. If you're sure that the value of the variable actually is the subtype you need, then you can use the `as` keyword to change the type. This is known as **type casting**.

Here's an example:

```
num someNumber = 3;
```

You have a number, and you want to check if it's even. You know that integers have an isEven property, so you attempt the following:

```
print(someNumber.isEven);
```

However, the compiler gives you an error:

```
The getter 'isEven' isn't defined for the type 'num'.
```

num is too general of a type to know anything about even or odd numbers. Only integers can be even or odd; so the issue is that num could potentially be a double at runtime, since num includes both double and int. In this case, though, you're sure that 3 is an integer, so you can cast someNumber to int.

```
final someInt = someNumber as int;
print(someInt.isEven);
```

The as keyword causes the compiler to recognize someInt as an int, so your code is now able to use the isEven property that belongs to the int type. Since 3 isn't even, Dart prints false.

You need to be careful with type casting, though. If you cast to the wrong type, you'll get a runtime error:

```
num someNumber = 3;
final someDouble = someNumber as double;
```

This will crash with the following message:

```
_CastError (type 'int' is not a subtype of type 'double' in type
cast)
```

The runtime type of someNumber is int, not double. In Dart, you're not allowed to cast to a sibling type, such as int to double. You can only cast down to a subtype.

If you do need to convert an int to a double at runtime, use the toDouble method that you saw earlier:

```
final someDouble = someNumber.toDouble();
```

Mini-exercises

1. Create a constant called `age1` and set it equal to 42. Create another constant called `age2` and set it equal to 21. Check that the type for both constants has been inferred correctly as `int` by hovering your mouse pointer over the variable names in VS Code.

2. Create a constant called `averageAge` and set it equal to the average of `age1` and `age2` using the operation `(age1 + age2) / 2`. Hover your mouse pointer over `averageAge` to check the type. Then check the result of `averageAge`. Why is it a `double` if the components are all `int`?

Strings

Numbers are essential in programming, but they aren't the only type of data you need to work with in your apps. Text is also a common data type, representing things such as people's names, their addresses, or even the complete text of a book. All of these are examples of text that an app might have to handle.

Most computer programming languages store text in a data type called a **string**. This chapter introduces you to strings, first by giving you background on the concept, and then by showing you how to use them in Dart.

How computers represent strings

Computers think of strings as a collection of individual **characters**. Numbers are the language of CPUs, and all code, in every programming language, can be reduced to raw numbers. Strings are no different.

That may sound very strange. How can characters be numbers? At its base, a computer needs to be able to translate a character into the computer's own language, and it does so by assigning each character a different number. This forms a two-way mapping from character to number that's called a **character set**.

When you press a character key on your keyboard, you are actually communicating the number of the character to the computer. Your computer converts that number into a picture of the character and finally, presents that picture to you.

Unicode

In isolation, a computer is free to choose whatever character set mapping it likes. If the computer wants the letter **a** to equal the number **10**, then so be it. But when computers start talking to each other, they need to use a common character set.

If two computers used different character sets, then when one computer transferred a string to the other, they would end up thinking the strings contained different characters.

There have been several standards over the years, but the most modern standard is **Unicode**. It defines the character set mapping that almost all computers use today.

> **Note**: You can read more about Unicode at its official website, <u>unicode.org</u>.

As an example, consider the word **cafe**. The Unicode standard tells us that the letters of this word should be mapped to numbers like so:

c	a	f	e
99	97	102	101

The number associated with each character is called a **code point**. So in the example above, **c** uses code point 99, **a** uses code point 97, and so on.

Of course, Unicode is not just for the simple Latin characters used in English, such as **c**, **a**, **f** and **e**. It also lets you map characters from languages around the world. The word **cafe**, as you're probably aware, is derived from French, in which it's written as **café**. Unicode maps these characters like so:

c	a	f	é
99	97	102	233

And here's an example using simplified Chinese characters that mean "I love you":

我	爱	你
25105	29233	20320

You're familiar with the small pictures called emojis that you can use when texting your friends. These pictures are, in fact, just normal characters and are also mapped by Unicode. For example:

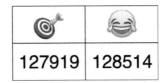

These are only two characters. The code points for them are very large numbers, but each is still only a single code point. The computer considers them no different than any other two characters.

> **Note**: The word "emoji" comes from the Japanese 絵文字, where "e" means picture and "moji" means character.

The numbers for each of the characters above were written in decimal notation, but you usually write Unicode code points in hexadecimal format. Here they are again in hex:

c	a	f	é	我	爱	你	🎯	😂
63	61	66	E9	6211	7231	4F60	1F3AF	1F602

Using base-16 makes the numbers more compact, easier to find in the Unicode character code charts and generally nicer to work with while programming.

Working with strings in Dart

Dart, like any good programming language, can work directly with strings. It does so through the `String` data type. In this section, you'll learn about this data type and how to work with it.

Strings and characters

You've already seen a Dart string back in Chapter 1 where you printed one:

```
print('Hello, Dart!');
```

You can extract that same string as a named variable:

```
var greeting = 'Hello, Dart!';
print(greeting);
```

The right-hand side of this expression is known as a **string literal**. Due to type inference, Dart knows that greeting is of type String. Since you used the var keyword, you're allowed to reassign the value of greeting as long as the new value is still a string.

```
var greeting = 'Hello, Dart!';
greeting = 'Hello, Flutter!';
```

Even though you changed the value of greeting here, you didn't modify the string itself. That's because strings are immutable in Dart. It's not like you replaced Dart in the first string with Flutter. No, you completely discarded the string 'Hello, Dart!' and replaced it with a whole new string whose value was 'Hello, Flutter!'.

Getting characters

> **Note**: The code examples below contain emoji characters that may be difficult to input on your keyboard. You can find all of them to conveniently copy-and-paste by opening **starter/bin/starter.dart** in the Chapter 3 supplemental materials for this book.
>
> Alternatively, you can use emojipedia.org with the following search terms: "dart", "Mongolia flag" and "man woman girl boy".

If you're familiar with other programming languages, you may be wondering about a Character or char type. Dart doesn't have that. Take a look at this example:

```
const letter = 'a';
```

So here, even though letter is only one character long, it's still of type String.

But strings are a collection of characters, right? What if you want to know the underlying number value of the character? No problem. Keep reading.

Dart strings are a collection of **UTF-16 code units**. UTF-16 is a way to encode Unicode values by using 16-bit numbers. If you want to find out what those UTF-16 codes are, you can do it like so:

```
var salutation = 'Hello!';
print(salutation.codeUnits);
```

This will print the following list of numbers in decimal notation:

```
[72, 101, 108, 108, 111, 33]
```

H is 72, **e** is 101, and so on.

These UTF-16 code units have the same value as Unicode code points for most of the characters you see on a day to day basis. However, 16 bits only give you 65,536 combinations, and believe it or not, there are more than 65,536 characters in the world! Remember the large numbers that the emojis had in the last section? You'll need more than 16 bits to represent those values.

UTF-16 has a special way of encoding code points higher than 65,536 by using two code units called **surrogate pairs**.

```
const dart = '🎯';
print(dart.codeUnits);
// [55356, 57263]
```

The code point for 🎯 is 127919, but the surrogate pair for that in UTF-16 is 55356 and 57263. No one wants to mess with surrogate pairs. It would be much nicer to just get Unicode code points directly. And you can! Dart calls them **runes**.

```
const dart = '🎯';
print(dart.runes);
// (127919)
```

Problem solved, right? If only it were.

Unicode grapheme clusters

Unfortunately, language is messy and so is Unicode. Have a look at this example:

```
const flag = '🇺🇸';
print(flag.runes);
// (127474, 127475)
```

Why are there two Unicode code points!? Well, it's because Unicode doesn't create a new code point every time there is a new country flag. It uses a pair of code points called **regional indicator symbols** to represent a flag. That's what you see in the example for the Mongolian flag above. 127474 is the code for the regional indicator symbol letter M, and 127475 is the code for the regional indicator symbol letter N. MN represents Mongolia.

If you thought that was complicated, look at this one:

```dart
const family = '👨‍👩‍👧‍👦';
print(family.runes);
// (128104, 8205, 128105, 8205, 128103, 8205, 128102)
```

That list of Unicode code points is a man, a woman, a girl and a boy all glued together with a characters called a **Zero Width Joiner** or **ZWJ**.

Now image trying to find the length of that string:

```dart
const family = '👨‍👩‍👧‍👦';

family.length;            // 11
family.codeUnits.length;  // 11
family.runes.length;      // 7
```

Getting the length of the string with `family.length` is equivalent to finding the number of UTF-16 code units: There are surrogate pairs for each of the four people plus the three ZWJ characters for a total of 11. Finding the runes gives you the seven Unicode code points that make up the emoji: man + ZWJ + woman + ZWJ + girl + ZWJ + boy. However, neither 11 nor 7 is what you'd expect. The family emoji looks like it's just one character. You'd think the length should be one!

When a string with multiple code points looks like a single character, this is known as a **user perceived character**. In technical terms it's called a **Unicode extended grapheme cluster**, or more commonly, just **grapheme cluster**.

Although the creators of Dart didn't support grapheme clusters in the language itself, they did make an add-on package that handles them.

Adding the characters package

This is a good opportunity to try out your first Pub package. In the root folder of your project, open **pubspec.yaml**.

> **Note:** If you don't see **pubspec.yaml**, go back to Chapter 1 to see how to create a new project. Alternatively, open the starter project that comes with the supplemental materials for Chapter 3 of this book.

Find the line that says `dependencies:` and add the `characters` package and version directly below that. It should look like this when you're done:

```
dependencies:
  characters: ^1.1.0
```

Indentation is important in `.yaml` files, so make sure to indent the package name with two spaces. The ^ carat character means that any version higher than or equal to `1.1.0` but lower than `2.0.0` is OK to use in your project. This is known as **semantic versioning**.

Now press **Command+S** on a Mac or **Control+S** on a PC to save the changes to **pubspec.yaml**. VS Code will automatically fetch the package from Pub. Alternatively, you can press the **Get Packages button** in the top right. It looks like a down arrow:

Both of these methods are equivalent to running the following command in the root folder of your project using the terminal:

```
dart pub get
```

> **Note**: Whenever you download and open a new Dart project that contains Pub packages, you'll need to run `dart pub get` first. This includes the final and challenge projects included in the supplemental materials for this chapter.

Now that you've added the `characters` package to your project, go back to your Dart code file and add the following import to the top of the page:

```
import 'package:characters/characters.dart';
```

Now you can use the code in the `characters` package to handle grapheme clusters. This package adds extra functionality to the String type.

```
const family = '👨‍👩‍👧‍👦';
family.characters.length; // 1
```

Aha! Now that's what you'd hope to see: just one character for the family emoji. The `characters` package extended `String` to include a collection of grapheme clusters called `characters`.

In your own projects, you can decide whether you want to work with UTF-16 code units, Unicode code points or grapheme clusters. However, as a general rule, you should strongly consider using grapheme clusters any time you're receiving text input from the outside world. That includes fetching data over the network or users typing things into your app.

Single-quotes vs. double-quotes

Dart allows you to use either single-quotes or double-quotes for string literals. Both of these are fine:

```
'I like cats'
"I like cats"
```

Although Dart doesn't have a recommended practice, the Flutter style guide does recommend using single-quotes, so this book will also follow that practice.

You might want to use double-quotes, though, if your string includes any apostrophes.

```
"my cat's food"
```

Otherwise you would need to use the backslash \ as an escape character so that Dart knows that the string isn't ending early:

```
'my cat\'s food'
```

Concatenation

You can do much more than create simple strings. Sometimes you need to manipulate a string, and one common way to do so is to combine it with another string. This is called **concatenation**...with no relation to the aforementioned felines.

In Dart, you can concatenate strings simply by using the addition operator. Just as you can add numbers, you can add strings:

```
var message = 'Hello' + ' my name is ';
const name = 'Ray';
message += name;
// 'Hello my name is Ray'
```

You need to declare `message` as a variable, rather than a constant, because you want to modify it. You can add string literals together, as in the first line, and you can add string variables or constants together, as in the third line.

If you find yourself doing a lot of concatenation, you should use a string buffer, which is more efficient.

```
final message = StringBuffer();
message.write('Hello');
message.write(' my name is ');
message.write('Ray');
message.toString();
// "Hello my name is Ray"
```

This creates a mutable location in memory where you can add to the string without having to create a new string for every change. When you're all done, you use `toString` to convert the string buffer to the `String` type. This is similar to what you saw with type conversion earlier with `toInt`.

Interpolation

You can also build up a string by using **interpolation**, which is a special Dart syntax that lets you build a string in a manner that's easy for other people reading your code to understand:

```
const name = 'Ray';
const introduction = 'Hello my name is $name';
// 'Hello my name is Ray'
```

This is much more readable than the example in the previous section. It's an extension of the string literal syntax, in which you replace certain parts of the string with other values. You add a dollar sign ($) in front of the value that you want to insert.

The syntax works in the same way to build a string from other data types such as numbers:

```
const oneThird = 1 / 3;
const sentence = 'One third is $oneThird.';
```

Here, you use a `double` for the interpolation. Your `sentence` constant will contain the following value:

```
One third is 0.3333333333333333.
```

Of course, it would actually take an infinite number of characters to represent one-third as a decimal, because it's a repeating decimal. You can control the number of decimal places shown on a `double` by using `toStringAsFixed` along with the number of decimal places to show:

```
final sentence = 'One third is ${oneThird.toStringAsFixed(3)}.';
```

There are a few items of interest here:

- You're requesting the string to show only three decimal places.

- Since you're performing an operation on `oneThird`, you need to surround the expression with curly braces after the dollar sign. This lets Dart know that the dot (`.`) after `oneThird` isn't just a regular period.

- The `sentence` variable needs to be `final` now instead of `const` because `toStringAsFixed(3)` is calculated at runtime.

Here's the result:

```
One third is 0.333.
```

Multi-line strings

Dart has a neat way to express strings that contain multiple lines, which can be rather useful when you need to use very long strings in your code.

You can support multi-line text like so:

```
const bigString = '''
You can have a string
that contains multiple
lines
by
doing this.''';
print(bigString);
```

The three single-quotes (''') signify that this is a multi-line string. Three double-quotes (""") would have done the same thing.

The example above will print the following:

```
You can have a string
that contains multiple
lines
by
doing this.
```

Notice that all of the newline locations are preserved. If you just want to use multiple lines in code but don't want the output string to contain newline characters, then you can surround each line with single-quotes:

```
const oneLine = 'This is only '
    'a single '
    'line '
    'at runtime.';
```

That's because Dart ignores whitespace outside of quoted text. This does the same thing as if you concatenated each of those lines with the + operator:

```
const oneLine = 'This is only ' +
    'a single ' +
    'line ' +
    'at runtime.';
```

Either way, this is what you get:

```
This is only a single line at runtime.
```

Like many languages, if you want to insert a newline character, you can use \n.

```
const twoLines = 'This is\ntwo lines.';
```

This gives:

```
This is
two lines.
```

However, sometimes you want to ignore any special characters that a string might contain. To do that, you can create a **raw string** by putting **r** in front of the string literal.

```
const rawString = r'My name \n is $name.';
```

And that's exactly what you get:

```
My name \n is $name.
```

Inserting characters from their codes

Similar to the way you can insert a newline character into a string using the \n escape sequence, you can also add Unicode characters if you know their codes. Take the following example:

```
print('I \u2764 Dart\u0021');
```

Here, you've used \u, followed by a four-digit hexadecimal code unit value. 2764 is the hex value for the heart emoji, and 21 is the hex value for an exclamation mark. Since 21 is only two digits, you pad it with extra zeros as 0021.

This prints:

I ♥ Dart!

For code points with values higher than hexadecimal FFFF, you need to surround the code with curly braces:

```
print('I love \u{1F3AF}');
```

This prints:

I love 🎯

In this way, you can form any Unicode string from its codes.

Mini-exercises

1. Create a string constant called `firstName` and initialize it to your first name. Also create a string constant called `lastName` and initialize it to your last name.

2. Create a string constant called `fullName` by adding the `firstName` and `lastName` constants together, separated by a space.

3. Using interpolation, create a string constant called `myDetails` that uses the `fullName` constant to create a string introducing yourself. For example, Ray Wenderlich's string would read: `Hello, my name is Ray Wenderlich.`

Object and dynamic types

Dart grew out of the desire to solve some problems inherent in JavaScript. JavaScript is a **dynamically-typed** language. Dynamic means that something can change, and for JavaScript that means the types can change at runtime.

Here is an example in JavaScript:

```
var myVariable = 42;
myVariable = "hello";
```

In JavaScript, the first line is a `number` and the second line a `string`. Changing the types on the fly like this is completely valid in JavaScript. While this may be convenient at times, it makes it *really* easy to write buggy code. For example, you may be erroneously thinking that `myVariable` is still a number, so you write the following code:

```
var answer = myVariable * 3; // runtime error
```

Oops! That's an error because `myVariable` is actually a string, and the computer doesn't know what to do with "hello" times 3. Not only is it an error, you won't even discover the error until you run the code.

You can totally prevent mistakes like that in Dart because it's an **optionally-typed** language. That means you can choose to use Dart as a dynamically typed language or as a **statically-typed** language. Static means that something *cannot* change; once you tell Dart what type a variable is, you're not allowed to change it anymore.

If you try to do the following in Dart:

```
var myVariable = 42;
myVariable = 'hello'; // compile-time error
```

The Dart compiler will immediately tell you that it's an error. That makes type errors trivial to detect.

As you saw in Chapter 2, the creators of Dart did include a dynamic type for those who wish write their programs in a dynamically-typed way.

```
dynamic myVariable = 42;
myVariable = 'hello'; // OK
```

In fact, this is the default if you use var and don't initialize your variable:

```
var myVariable; // defaults to dynamic
myVariable = 42;      // OK
myVariable = 'hello'; // OK
```

While dynamic is built into the system, it's more of a concession rather than an encouragement to use it. You should still embrace static typing in your code as it will prevent you from making silly mistakes.

If you need to explicitly say that any type is allowed, you should consider using the Object? type.

```
Object? myVariable = 42;
myVariable = 'hello'; // OK
```

At runtime, Object? and dynamic behave nearly the same. However, when you explicitly declare a variable as Object?, you're telling everyone that you generalized your variable on purpose, and that they'll need to check its type at runtime if they want to do anything specific with it. Using dynamic, on the other hand, is more like saying you don't know what the type is; you're telling people they can do what they like with this variable, but it's completely on them if their code crashes.

> **Note:** You may be wondering what that question mark at the end of Object? is. That means that the type can include the null value. You'll learn more about nullability in Chapter 7.

Challenges

Before moving on, here are some challenges to test your knowledge of types and operations. It's best if you try to solve them yourself, but solutions are available with the supplementary materials for this book if you get stuck.

As described in the **Getting characters** section above, you can find the required emoji characters in the **starter** project or from emojipedia.org where you can use the search terms "Chad flag", "Romania flag" and "thumbs up dark skin tone".

Challenge 1: Teacher's grading

You're a teacher, and in your class, attendance is worth 20% of the grade, the homework is worth 30% and the exam is worth 50%. Your student got 90 points for her attendance, 80 points for her homework and 94 points on her exam. Calculate her grade as an integer percentage rounded down.

Challenge 2: Same same, but different

This string has two flags that look the same. But they aren't! One of them is the flag of Chad and the other is the flag of Romania.

```
const twoCountries = '🇹🇩🇷🇴';
```

Which is which?

Hint: Romania's regional indicator sequence is RO, and R is 127479 in decimal. Chad, which is *Tishād* in Arabic and *Tchad* in French, has a regional indicator sequence of TD. Sequence letter T is 127481 in decimal.

Challenge 3: How many?

Given the following string:

```
const vote = 'Thumbs up! 👍';
```

- How many UTF-16 code units are there?

- How many Unicode code points are there?

- How many Unicode grapheme clusters are there?

Challenge 4: Find the error

What is wrong with the following code?

```
const name = 'Ray';
name += ' Wenderlich';
```

Challenge 5: What type?

What's the type of `value`?

```
const value = 10 / 2;
```

Challenge 6: In summary

What is the value of the constant named `summary`?

```
const number = 10;
const multiplier = 5;
final summary = '$number \u00D7 $multiplier = ${number *
multiplier}';
```

Key points

- Type conversion allows you to convert values of one type into another.

- When doing operations with basic arithmetic operators (+, −, *, /) and mixed types, the result will be a double.

- Type inference allows you to omit the type when Dart can figure it out.

- Unicode is the standard representation for mapping characters to numbers.

- Dart uses UTF-16 values known as code units to encode Unicode strings.

- A single mapping in Unicode is called a code point, which is known as a rune in Dart.

- User-perceived characters may be composed of one or more code points and are called grapheme characters.

- You can combine strings by using the addition operator.

- You can make multi-line strings using three single-quotes or double quotes.

- You can use string interpolation to build a string in-place.

- Dart is an optionally-typed language. While it's preferable to choose statically-typed variables, you may write Dart code in a dynamically-typed way by explicitly adding the dynamic type annotation in front of variables.

Chapter 4: Control Flow

By Jonathan Sande & Matt Galloway

When writing a computer program, you need to be able to tell the computer what to do in different scenarios. For example, a calculator app would need to perform one action if the user taps the addition button, and another action if the user taps the subtraction button.

In computer programming terms, this concept is known as **control flow**, because you can control the flow of decisions the code makes at multiple points. In this chapter, you'll learn how to make decisions and repeat tasks in your programs.

Making comparisons

You've already encountered a few different Dart types, such as `int`, `double` and `String`. Each of those types is a data structure which is designed to hold a particular type of data. The `int` type is for whole numbers while the `double` type is for decimal numbers. `String`, by comparison, is useful for storing textual information.

A new way of structuring information, though, requires a new data type. Consider the answers to the following questions:

- Is the door open?

- Do pigs fly?

- Is that the same shirt you were wearing yesterday?

- Is the traffic light red?

- Are you older than your grandmother?

- Does this make me look fat?

These are all yes-no questions. If you want to store the answers in a variable, you could use strings like `'yes'` and `'no'`. You could even use integers where 0 means no and 1 means yes. The problem with that, though, is what happens when you get 42 or `'celery'`? It would be better to avoid any ambiguity and have a type in which the only possible values are yes and no.

Boolean values

Dart has a data type just for this. It's called `bool`, which is short for **Boolean**. A Boolean value can have one of two states. While in general you could refer to the states as yes and no, on and off, or 1 and 0, most programming languages, Dart included, call them **true** and **false**.

The word Boolean was named after George Boole, the man who pioneered an entire field of mathematics around the concept of true and false. Since computers themselves are based on electrical circuits which can be in a binary state of on or off, Boolean math is fundamental to computer science.

When programming in a high level language like Dart, you don't need to understand all of the Boolean logic that's happening at the circuit level, but there's still a lot about Boolean math you can apply to decision making in your own code.

To start your exploration of Booleans in Dart, create some Boolean variables like so:

```
const bool yes = true;
const bool no = false;
```

Because of Dart's type inference, you can leave off the type annotation:

```
const yes = true;
const no = false;
```

In the code above, you use the keywords `true` and `false` to set the state of each Boolean constant.

Boolean operators

Booleans are commonly used to compare values. For example, you may have two values and you want to know if they're equal. Either they *are* equal, which would be `true`, or they *aren't* equal, which would be `false`.

Next you'll see how to make that comparison in Dart.

Testing equality

You can test for equality using the **equality operator**, which is denoted by ==, that is, two equals signs.

Write the following line:

```
const doesOneEqualTwo = (1 == 2);
```

Dart infers that `doesOneEqualTwo` is a `bool`. Clearly, 1 does not equal 2, and therefore `doesOneEqualTwo` will be `false`. Confirm that result by printing the value:

```
print(doesOneEqualTwo);
```

Sometimes you need parentheses to tell Dart what should happen first. However, the parentheses in that last example were there only for readability, that is, to show you that the two objects being compared were 1 and 2. You could have also written it like so:

```
const doesOneEqualTwo = 1 == 2;
```

Note: You may use the equality operator to compare `int` to `double`, since they both belong to the num type.

Testing inequality

You can also find out if two values are *not* equal using the != operator:

```
const doesOneNotEqualTwo = (1 != 2);
```

This time, the result of the comparison is true because 1 does not equal 2, so doesOneNotEqualTwo will be true.

The prefix ! operator, also called the **not-operator** or **bang operator**, toggles true to false and false to true. Another way to write the above is:

```
const alsoTrue = !(1 == 2);
```

Because 1 does not equal 2, (1 == 2) is false, and then ! flips it to true.

Testing greater and less than

There are two other operators to help you compare two values and determine if a value is greater than (>) or less than (<) another value. You know these from mathematics:

```
const isOneGreaterThanTwo = (1 > 2);
const isOneLessThanTwo = (1 < 2);
```

It's not rocket science to work out that isOneGreaterThanTwo will equal false and that isOneLessThanTwo will equal true.

The <= operator lets you test if a value is *less than or equal to* another value. It's a combination of < and ==, and will therefore return true if the first value is less than, or equal to, the second value.

```
print(1 <= 2); // true
print(2 <= 2); // true
```

Similarly, the >= operator lets you test if a value is *greater than or equal to* another value.

```
print(2 >= 1); // true
print(2 >= 2); // true
```

Boolean logic

Each of the examples above tests just one condition. When George Boole invented the Boolean, he had much more planned for it than these humble beginnings. He invented Boolean logic, which lets you combine multiple conditions to form a result.

AND operator

Ray would like to go cycling in the park with Vicki this weekend. It's a little uncertain whether they can go, though. There's a chance that it might rain. Also, Vicky says she can't go unless she finishes up the art project she's working on. So Ray and Vicki will go cycling in the park if it's sunny *and* Vicki finishes her work.

When two conditions need to be true in order for the result to be true, this is an example of a Boolean **AND** operation. If both input Booleans are true, then the result is true. Otherwise, the result is false. If it rains, Ray won't go cycling with Vicki. Or if Vicki doesn't finish her work, they won't go cycling, either.

In Dart, the operator for Boolean AND is written &&, used like so:

```
const isSunny = true;
const isFinished = true;
const willGoCycling = isSunny && isFinished;
```

Print `willGoCycling` and you'll see that it's `true`. If either `isSunny` or `isFinished` were `false`, then `willGoCycling` would also be `false`.

OR operator

Vicki would like to draw a platypus, but she needs a model. She could either travel to Australia *or* she could find a photograph on the internet. If only one of two conditions need to be true in order for the result to be true, this is an example of a Boolean **OR** operation. The only instance where the result would be false is if *both* input Booleans were false. If Vicki doesn't go to Australia and she also doesn't find a photograph on the internet, then she won't draw a platypus.

In Dart, the operator for Boolean OR is written ||, used like so:

```
const willTravelToAustralia = true;
const canFindPhoto = false;
const canDrawPlatypus = willTravelToAustralia || canFindPhoto;
```

Print `canDrawPlatypus` to see that its value is `true`. If both values on the right were `false`, then `canDrawPlatypus` would be `false`. If both were `true`, then `canDrawPlatypus` would still be `true`.

Operator precedence

As was the case in the Ray and Vicki examples above, Boolean logic is usually applied to multiple conditions. When you want to determine if two conditions are true, you use AND, while if you only care whether one of the two conditions is true, you use OR.

Here are a few more examples:

```
const andTrue = 1 < 2 && 4 > 3;
const andFalse = 1 < 2 && 3 > 4;
const orTrue = 1 < 2 || 3 > 4;
const orFalse = 1 == 2 || 3 == 4;
```

Each of these tests two separate conditions, combining them with either AND or OR.

It's also possible to use Boolean logic to combine more than two comparisons. For example, you can form a complex comparison like so:

```
3 > 4 && 1 < 2 || 1 < 4
```

But now it gets a little confusing. You have three conditions with two different logical operators. With the comparisons simplified, you have the following form:

```
false && true || true
```

Depending on the order you perform the AND and OR operations, you get different results. If you evaluate AND first, the whole expression is `true`, while if you evaluate OR first, the whole expression is `false`.

This is where **operator precedence** comes in. The following list shows the order that Dart uses to evaluate expressions containing comparison and logical operators:

Operators higher in the list are executed before operators lower in the list. You can see that && has a higher precedence than ||. So back to case from before:

```
false && true || true
```

First Dart will evaluate `false && true`, which is `false`. Then Dart will take that `false` to evaluate `false || true`, which is `true`. Thus the whole expression evaluates to `true`.

Overriding precedence with parentheses

If you want to override the default operator precedence, you can put parentheses around the parts Dart should evaluate first.

Compare the following two expressions:

```
3 > 4 && (1 < 2 || 1 < 4)  // false
(3 > 4 && 1 < 2) || 1 < 4  // true
```

The parentheses in the first line force Dart to do the OR operation before the AND operation, even though that isn't the default order. This results in the entire expression evaluating to `false` instead of `true`, as it would have if you hadn't used parentheses.

Even when parentheses are not strictly required, as in the second of the two expressions above, they can still help to make the code more readable. For this reason, it's usually a good idea to use parentheses when you're performing a logical operation on more than two conditions.

String equality

Sometimes you'll want to determine if two strings are equal. For example, a children's game of naming an animal in a photo would need to determine if the player answered correctly.

In Dart, you can compare strings using the standard equality operator, ==, in exactly the same way as you compare numbers. For example:

```
const guess = 'dog';
const dogEqualsCat = guess == 'cat';
```

Here, `dogEqualsCat` is a Boolean, which in this case is `false` because the string `'dog'` does not equal the string `'cat'`.

Mini-exercises

1. Create a constant called `myAge` and set it to your age. Then, create a constant named `isTeenager` that uses Boolean logic to determine if the age denotes someone in the age range of 13 to 19.

2. Create another constant named `maryAge` and set it to `30`. Then, create a constant named `bothTeenagers` that uses Boolean logic to determine if both you and Mary are teenagers.

3. Create a `String` constant named `reader` and set it to your name. Create another `String` constant named `ray` and set it to `'Ray Wenderlich'`. Create a Boolean constant named `rayIsReader` that uses string equality to determine if `reader` and `ray` are equal.

Now that you understand Boolean logic, you're going to use that knowledge to make decisions in your code.

The if statement

The first and most common way of controlling the flow of a program is through the use of an **if statement**, which allows the program to do something only if a certain condition is true. For example, consider the following:

```
if (2 > 1) {
  print('Yes, 2 is greater than 1.');
}
```

This is a simple `if` statement. The **condition**, which is always a **Boolean expression**, is the part within the parentheses that follows the `if` statement. If the condition is `true`, then the `if` statement will execute the code between the braces. If the condition is `false`, then the `if` statement *won't* execute the code between the braces.

Obviously, the condition `(2 > 1)` is `true`, so when you run that you'll see:

```
Yes, 2 is greater than 1.
```

The else clause

You can extend an `if` statement to provide code to run in the event that the condition turns out to be `false`. This is known as the **else clause**.

Here's an example:

```
const animal = 'Fox';
if (animal == 'Cat' || animal == 'Dog') {
  print('Animal is a house pet.');
} else {
  print('Animal is not a house pet.');
}
```

If animal equals either 'Cat' or 'Dog', then the statement will execute the first block of code. If animal does *not* equal either 'Cat' or 'Dog', then the statement will run the block inside the else clause of the if statement.

Run that code and you'll see the following in the debug console:

```
Animal is not a house pet.
```

Else-if chains

You can go even further with if statements. Sometimes you want to check one condition, and then check another condition if the first condition isn't true. This is where else-if comes into play, nesting another if statement in the else clause of a previous if statement.

You can use it like so:

```
const trafficLight = 'yellow';
var command = '';
if (trafficLight == 'red') {
  command = 'Stop';
} else if (trafficLight == 'yellow') {
  command = 'Slow down';
} else if (trafficLight == 'green') {
  command = 'Go';
} else {
  command = 'INVALID COLOR!';
}
print(command);
```

In this example, the first if statement will check if trafficLight is equal to 'red'. Since it's not, the next if statement will check if trafficLight is equal to 'yellow'. It is equal to 'yellow', so no check will be made for the case of 'green'.

Run the code and it will print the following:

```
Slow down
```

These nested if statements test multiple conditions, one by one, until a true condition is found. Only the code associated with the first true condition encountered will be executed, regardless of whether there are subsequent else-if conditions that evaluate to true. In other words, the order of your conditions matters!

You can add an else clause at the end to handle the case where none of the conditions are true. This else clause is optional if you don't need it. In this example, you *do* need the else clause to ensure that command has a value by the time you print it out.

Variable scope

if statements introduce a new concept called **scope**. Scope is the extent to which a variable can be seen throughout your code. Dart uses curly braces as the boundary markers in determining a variable's scope. If you define a variable inside a pair of curly braces, then you're not allowed to use that variable outside of those braces.

To see how this works, replace the main function with the following code:

```dart
const global = 'Hello, world';

void main() {
  const local = 'Hello, main';

  if (2 > 1) {
    const insideIf = 'Hello, anybody?';

    print(global);
    print(local);
    print(insideIf);
  }

  print(global);
  print(local);
  print(insideIf); // Not allowed!
}
```

Note the following points:

• There are three variables: global, local and insideIf.

• There are two sets of nested curly braces, one for the body of main and one for the body of the if statement.

- The variable named global is defined outside of the main function and outside of any curly braces. That makes it a **top-level variable**, which means it has a global scope. That is, it's visible everywhere in the file. You can see print(global) references it both in the if statement body and in the main function body.

- The variable named local is defined inside the body of the main function. This makes it a **local variable** and it has local scope. It's visible inside the main function, including inside the if statement, but local is not visible outside of the main function.

- The variable named insideIf is defined inside the body of the if statement. That means insideIf is only visible within the scope defined by the if statement's curly braces.

Since the final print statement is trying to reference insideIf outside of its scope, Dart gives you the following error:

```
Undefined name 'insideIf'.
```

Delete that final print statement to get rid of the error.

As a general rule, you should make your variables have the smallest scope that they can get by with. Another way to say that is, define your variables as close to where you use them as possible. Doing so makes their purpose more clear, and it also prevents you from using or changing them in places where you shouldn't.

The ternary conditional operator

You've worked with operators that have two operands. For example, in (myAge > 16), the two operands are myAge and 16. But there's also an operator that takes three operands: the **ternary conditional operator**. It's strangely related to if statements — you'll see why this is in just a bit.

Let's take an example of telling a student whether their exam score is passing or not. Write an if-else statement to achieve this:

```
const score = 83;

String message;
if (score >= 60) {
  message = 'You passed';
} else {
  message = 'You failed';
}
```

That's pretty clear, but it's a lot of code. Wouldn't it be nice if you could shrink this to just a couple of lines? Well, you can, thanks to the ternary conditional operator!

The ternary conditional operator takes a condition and returns one of two values, depending on whether the condition is true or false. The syntax is as follows:

```
(condition) ? valueIfTrue : valueIfFalse;
```

Use the ternary conditional operator to rewrite your long code block above, like so:

```
const score = 83;
const message = (score >= 60) ? 'You passed' : 'You failed';
```

In this example, the condition to evaluate is `score >= 60`. If the condition is `true`, the result assigned to `message` will be `'You passed'`; if the condition is `false`, the result will instead be `'You failed'`. Since 83 is greater than 60, the student receives good news.

The ternary conditional operator makes basic `if-else` statements much more compact, which in turn can make your code more readable.

However, for situations where using this operator makes your code *less* readable, then stick with the full `if-else` statement. Readability is always more important than fancy programming tricks that give the same result.

Mini-exercises

1. Create a constant named `myAge` and initialize it with your age. Write an `if` statement to print out "Teenager" if your age is between 13 and 19, and "Not a teenager" if your age is not between 13 and 19.

2. Use a ternary conditional operator to replace the `else-if` statement that you used above. Set the result to a variable named `answer`.

Switch statements

An alternate way to handle control flow, especially for multiple conditions, is with a `switch` statement. The `switch` statement takes the following form:

```
switch (variable) {
  case value1:
    // code
    break;
```

```
  case value2:
    // code
    break;

    ...

  default:
    // code
}
```

There are a few different keywords, so here are what they mean:

- **switch**: Based on the value of the variable in parentheses, which can be an int, String or compile-time constant, switch will redirect the program control to one of the case values that follow.

- **case**: Each case keyword takes a value and compares that value using == to the variable after the switch keyword. You add as many case statements as there are values to check. When there's a match Dart will run the code that follows the colon.

- **break**: The break keyword tells Dart to exit the switch statement because the code in the case block is finished.

- **default**: If none of the case values match the switch variable, then the code after default will be executed.

The following sections will provide more detailed examples of switch statements.

Replacing else-if chains

Using if statements are convenient when you have one or two conditions, but the syntax can be a little verbose when you have a lot of conditions. Check out the following example:

```
const number = 3;
if (number == 0) {
  print('zero');
} else if (number == 1) {
  print('one');
} else if (number == 2) {
  print('two');
} else if (number == 3) {
  print('three');
} else if (number == 4) {
  print('four');
} else {
```

```
    print('something else');
  }
```

Run that code and you'll see that it gets the job done — it prints three as expected. The wordiness of the else-if lines make the code kind of hard to read, though.

Rewrite the code above using a switch statement:

```
const number = 3;
switch (number) {
  case 0:
    print('zero');
    break;
  case 1:
    print('one');
    break;
  case 2:
    print('two');
    break;
  case 3:
    print('three');
    break;
  case 4:
    print('four');
    break;
  default:
    print('something else');
}
```

Execute this code and you'll get the same result of three again. However, the code looks cleaner than the else-if chain because you didn't need to include the explicit condition check for every case.

> **Note**: In Dart, switch statements don't support ranges like number > 5. Only == equality checking is allowed. If your conditions involve ranges, then you should use if statements.

Switching on strings

A switch statement also works with strings. Try the following example:

```
const weather = 'cloudy';
switch (weather) {
  case 'sunny':
    print('Put on sunscreen.');
    break;
```

```
    case 'snowy':
      print('Get your skis.');
      break;
    case 'cloudy':
    case 'rainy':
      print('Bring an umbrella.');
      break;
    default:
      print("I'm not familiar with that weather.");
  }
```

Run the code above and the following will be printed in the console:

```
Bring an umbrella.
```

In this example, the `'cloudy'` case was completely empty, with no `break` statement. Therefore, the code "falls through" to the `'rainy'` case. This means that if the value is equal to either `'cloudy'` or `'rainy'`, then the `switch` statement will execute the same case.

Enumerated types

Enumerated types, also known as **enums**, play especially well with `switch` statements. You can use them to define your own type with a finite number of options.

Consider the previous example with the `switch` statement about weather. You're expecting `weather` to contain a string with a recognized weather word. But it's conceivable that you might get something like this from one of your users:

```
const weather = 'I like turtles.';
```

You'd be like, "What? What are you even talking about?"

That's what the `default` case was there for — to catch all the weird stuff that gets through. Wouldn't it be nice to make weird stuff impossible, though? That's where enums come in.

Create the enum as follows, placing it outside of the `main` function:

```
enum Weather {
  sunny,
  snowy,
  cloudy,
  rainy,
}
```

This enum defines four different kinds of weather. Yes, yes, you can probably think of more kinds than that; feel free to add them yourself. But please don't make `iLikeTurtles` an option. Separate each of the values with a comma.

> **Formatting tip:** If you like the enum options listed in a vertical column as they are above, make sure the final item in the list has a comma after it. On the other hand, if you like them laid out horizontally, remove the comma after the last item. Once you've done that, pressing **Shift+Option+F** on a Mac or **Shift+Alt+F** on a PC in VS Code will auto-format it to your preferred style:
>
> ```
> enum Weather { sunny, snowy, cloudy, rainy }
> ```
>
> This formatting trick works with many kinds of lists in Dart.

Naming enums

When creating an enum in Dart, it's customary to write the enum name with an initial capital letter, as `Weather` was written in the example above. The values of an enum should use `lowerCamelCase` unless you have a special reason to do otherwise.

Switching on enums

Now that you have the `enum` defined, you can use a `switch` statement to handle all the possibilities, like so:

```
const weatherToday = Weather.cloudy;
switch (weatherToday) {
  case Weather.sunny:
    print('Put on sunscreen.');
    break;
  case Weather.snowy:
    print('Get your skis.');
    break;
  case Weather.cloudy:
  case Weather.rainy:
    print('Bring an umbrella.');
    break;
}
```

As before, this will print the following message:

```
Bring an umbrella.
```

Notice that there was no default case this time since you handled every single possibility. In fact, Dart will warn you if you leave one of the enum items out. That'll save you some time chasing bugs.

Enum values and indexes

Before leaving the topic of enums, there's one more thing to note. If you try to print an enum, you'll get its value:

```
print(weatherToday);
// Weather.cloudy
```

Unlike some languages, a Dart enum isn't an integer. However, you can get the index, or ordinal placement, of a value in the enum like so:

```
final index = weatherToday.index;
```

Since cloudy is the third value in the enum, the zero-based index is 2.

Avoiding the overuse of switch statements

Switch statements, or long else-if chains, can be a convenient way to handle a long list of conditions. If you're a beginning programmer, go ahead and use them; they're easy to use and understand.

However, if you're an intermediate programmer and still find yourself using switch statements a lot, there's a good chance you could replace some of them with more advanced programming techniques that will make your code easier to maintain. If you're interested, do a web search for **refactoring switch statements with polymorphism** and read a few articles about it.

Mini-exercises

1. Make an enum called AudioState and give it values to represent playing, paused and stopped states.

2. Create a constant called audioState and give it an AudioState value. Write a switch statement that prints a message based on the value.

Loops

In the first three chapters of this book, your code ran from the top of the `main` function to the bottom, and then it was finished. With the addition of `if` statements in this chapter, you gave your code the opportunity to make decisions. However, it's still running from top to bottom, albeit following different branches.

Rather than just running through a set of instructions once, it's often useful to repeat tasks. Think about all the repetitious things you do every day:

- **Breathing**: Breathe in, breathe out, breathe in, breathe out...

- **Walking**: Right leg forward, left leg forward, right leg forward, left leg forward...

- **Eating**: Spoon up, spoon down, chew, chew, chew, swallow, repeat...

Computer programming is just as full of repetitive actions as your life is. The way you can accomplish them are by using **loops**. Dart, like many programming languages, has `while` loops and `for` loops. You'll learn how to make them in the following sections.

While loops

A **while loop** repeats a block of code as long as a Boolean condition is true. You create a while loop like so:

```
while (condition) {
  // loop code
}
```

The loop checks the condition on every iteration. If the condition is `true`, then the loop executes and moves on to another iteration. If the condition is `false`, then the loop stops. Just like `if` statements, `while` loops introduce a scope because of their curly braces.

The simplest `while` loop takes this form:

```
while (true) { }
```

This is a `while` loop that never ends, because the condition is always `true`. Of course, you would never write such a `while` loop, because your program would spin forever! This situation is known as an **infinite loop**, and while it might not cause your program to crash, it will very likely cause your computer to freeze.

Here's a (somewhat) more useful example of a while loop:

```
var sum = 1;
while (sum < 10) {
    sum += 4;
    print(sum);
}
```

Run that to see the result. The loop executes as follows:

- Before 1st iteration: sum = 1, loop condition = true

- After 1st iteration: sum = 5, loop condition = true

- After 2nd iteration: sum = 9, loop condition = true

- After 3rd iteration: sum = 13, loop condition = false

After the third iteration, the sum variable is 13, and therefore the loop condition of sum < 10 becomes false. At this point, the loop stops.

Do-while loops

A variant of the while loop is called the do-while loop. It differs from the while loop in that the condition is evaluated at the *end* of the loop rather than at the beginning. Thus, the body of a do-while loop is always executed at least once.

You construct a do-while loop like this:

```
do {
    // loop code
} while (condition)
```

Whatever statements appear inside the braces will be executed. Finally, if the while condition after the closing brace is true, you jump back up to the beginning and repeat the loop.

Here's the example from the last section, but using a do-while loop:

```
sum = 1;
do {
    sum += 4;
    print(sum);
} while (sum < 10);
```

In this example, the outcome is the same as before.

Comparing while and do-while loops

It isn't always the case that `while` loops and `do-while` loops will give the same result. For example, here's a `while` loop where `sum` starts at **11**:

```
sum = 11;
while (sum < 10) {
  sum += 4;
}
print(sum);
```

Since the initial condition is `false`, the loop never executes. Run that code and you'll see that `sum` remains **11**.

On the other hand, check out a similar `do-while` loop:

```
sum = 11;
do {
  sum += 4;
} while (sum < 10);
print(sum);
```

Run this and you'll find the `sum` at the end to be **15**. This is because the `do-while` loop executed the body of the loop before checking the condition.

Breaking out of a loop

Sometimes you'll need to break out of a loop early. You can do this using the `break` statement, just as you did from inside the `switch` statement earlier. This immediately stops the execution of the loop and continues on to the code that follows the loop.

For example, consider the following `while` loop:

```
sum = 1;
while (true) {
  sum += 4;
  if (sum > 10) {
    break;
  }
}
```

Here, the loop condition is `true`, so the loop would normally iterate forever. However, the `break` means the `while` loop will exit once the sum is greater than **10**.

You've now seen how to write the same loop in different ways. This demonstrates that in computer programming there are often many ways to achieve the same result. You should choose the method that's easiest to read and that conveys your intent in the best way possible. This is an approach you'll internalize with enough time and practice.

A random interlude

A common need in programming is to be able to generate random numbers. And Dart provides this functionality in the dart:math library, which is pretty handy!

As an example, imagine an application that needs to simulate rolling a die. You may want to do something in your code until a six is rolled, and then stop. Now that you know about while loops, you can do that with the Random feature.

First import the dart:math library at the top of your Dart file:

```
import 'dart:math';
```

Then create the while loop like so:

```
final random = Random();
while (random.nextInt(6) + 1 != 6) {
  print('Not a six!');
}
print('Finally, you got a six!');
```

Random is a class to help with random numbers, and nextInt is a method that generates a random integer between 0 and one less than the maximum value you give it, in this case, 6. Since you want a number between 1 and 6, not 0 to 5, you must add 1 to the random number in the while loop condition.

> **Note:** You'll learn more about classes and methods in Chapter 6.

Run the loop and you'll get a variable number of outputs:

```
Not a six!
Not a six!
Finally, you got a six!
```

In this case it was only two loops before a lucky six was rolled. You probably had a different number of rolls, though.

For loops

In addition to `while` loops, Dart has another type of loop called a **for loop**. This is probably the most common loop you'll see, and you use it to run a block of code a set number of times. In this section you'll learn about C-style `for` loops, and in the next section, about `for-in` loops.

Here's a simple example of a **C-style for loop** in Dart:

```
for (var i = 0; i < 5; i++) {
  print(i);
}
```

If you have some prior programming experience, this C programming language style `for` loop probably looks very familiar to you. If not, though, the first line would be confusing. Here's a summary of the three parts between the parentheses and separated by semicolons:

- `var i = 0` (**initialization**): Before the loop starts, you create a counter variable to keep track of how many times you've looped. You could call the variable anything, but `i` is commonly used as an abbreviation for *index*. You then initialize it with some value; in this case, `0`.

- `i < 5` (**condition**): This is the condition that the `for` loop will check before every iteration of the loop. If it's `true`, then it will run the code inside the braces. But if it's `false`, then the loop will end.

- `i++` (**action**): The action runs at the end of every iteration, usually to update the loop index value. It's common to increment by 1 using `i++` but you could just as easily use `i += 2` to increment by 2 or `i--` to decrement by 1.

Run the code above and you'll see the following output:

```
0
1
2
3
4
```

The counter index `i` started at `0` and continued until it equaled 5. At that point the `for` loop condition `i < 5` was no longer `true`, so the loop exited before running the `print` statement again.

The continue keyword

Sometimes you want to skip an iteration only for a certain condition. You can do that using the `continue` keyword. Have a look at the following example:

```
for (var i = 0; i < 5; i++) {
  if (i == 2) {
    continue;
  }
  print(i);
}
```

This example is similar to the last one, but this time, when i is 2, the `continue` keyword will tell the `for` loop to immediately go on to the next iteration. The rest of the code in the block won't run on this iteration.

This is what you'll see:

```
0
1
3
4
```

No 2 here!

For-in loops

There's another type of `for` loop that has simpler syntax; it's called a **for-in loop**. It doesn't have any sort of index or counter variable associated with it, but it makes iterating over a collection very convenient.

You haven't formally learned about collections yet in this book; you'll get to them in Chapter 8. Dart collections aren't that difficult to learn, though, especially if you're familiar with them from other languages. In fact, Chapter 3 already snuck some in. Remember? Strings are a collection of characters.

When you get the runes from a string, that gives you a collection of Unicode code points. You can use that knowledge now to loop over the code points in a string like so:

```
const myString = 'I ♥ Dart';

for (var codePoint in myString.runes) {
  print(String.fromCharCode(codePoint));
}
```

Here's what's happening:

- `myString.runes` is a collection of all the code points in `myString`.

- The `in` keyword tells the `for-in` loop to iterate over the collection in order, and on each iteration, to assign the current code point to the `codePoint` variable. Since `runes` is a collection of integers, `codePoint` is inferred to be an `int`.

- Inside the braces you use `String.fromCharCode` to convert the code point integer back into a string.

- In terms of scope, the `codePoint` variable is only visible inside the scope of the `for-in` loop, which means it's not available outside of the loop.

Run the code and you'll see the following output:

```
I

♥

D
a
r
t
```

For-each loops

You can sometimes simplify `for-in` loops even more with the `forEach` method that is available to collections.

Even though you haven't learned about Dart collections in depth yet, here's another one for you:

```
const myNumbers = [1, 2, 3];
```

This is a comma-separated list of integers surrounded by square brackets.

Loop through each of the elements in that list by using `forEach` like so:

```
myNumbers.forEach((number) => print(number));
```

The part inside the `forEach` parentheses is a function, where => is **arrow syntax** that points to the statement that the function runs.

It has exactly the same meaning as the following, which uses { } braces instead of arrow syntax:

```
myNumbers.forEach((number) {
    print(number);
});
```

You might be wondering why number isn't declared anywhere. That's because Dart automatically gives number the type that's inside the collection; in this case, int.

Don't worry if this still looks strange to you. You'll learn all about functions in the next chapter. Consider this a sneak preview.

Run either of the forEach examples above and you'll see the same results:

```
1
2
3
```

Mini-exercises

1. Create a variable named counter and set it equal to 0. Create a while loop with the condition counter < 10. The loop body should print out "counter is X" (where X is replaced with the value of counter) and then increment counter by 1.

2. Write a for loop starting at 1 and ending with 10 inclusive. Print the square of each number.

3. Write a for-in loop to iterate over the following collection of numbers. Print the square root of each number.

```
const numbers = [1, 2, 4, 7];
```

4. Repeat Mini-exercise 3 using a forEach loop.

Challenges

Before moving on, here are some challenges to test your knowledge of control flow. It's best if you try to solve them yourself, but solutions are available in the challenge folder if you get stuck.

Challenge 1: Find the error

What's wrong with the following code?

```
const firstName = 'Bob';
if (firstName == 'Bob') {
  const lastName = 'Smith';
} else if (firstName == 'Ray') {
  const lastName = 'Wenderlich';
}
final fullName = firstName + ' ' + lastName;
```

Challenge 2: Boolean challenge

In each of the following statements, what is the value of the Boolean expression?

```
true && true
false || false
(true && 1 != 2) || (4 > 3 && 100 < 1)
((10 / 2) > 3) && ((10 % 2) == 0)
```

Challenge 3: Next power of two

Given a number, determine the next power of two above or equal to that number. Powers of two are the numbers in the sequence of 2^1, 2^2, 2^3, and so on. You may also recognize the series as 1, 2, 4, 8, 16, 32, 64...

Challenge 4: Fibonacci

Calculate the *n*th Fibonacci number. The Fibonacci sequence starts with 1, then 1 again, and then all subsequent numbers in the sequence are simply the previous two values in the sequence added together (1, 1, 2, 3, 5, 8...). You can get a refresher here: https://en.wikipedia.org/wiki/Fibonacci_number

Challenge 5: How many times?

In the following `for` loop, what will be the value of `sum`, and how many iterations will happen?

```
var sum = 0;
for (var i = 0; i <= 5; i++) {
  sum += i;
}
```

Challenge 6: The final countdown

Print a countdown from 10 to 0.

Challenge 7: Print a sequence

Print the sequence `0.0, 0.1, 0.2, 0.3, 0.4, 0.5, 0.6, 0.7, 0.8, 0.9, 1.0`.

Key points

- You use the Boolean data type `bool` to represent `true` and `false`.

- The comparison operators, all of which return a Boolean, are:

Name	Operator
Equal	==
Not equal	!=
Less than	<
Greater than	>
Less than or equal	<=
Greater than or equal	>=

- You can use Boolean logic (&& and ||) to combine comparison conditions.

- You use `if` statements to make simple decisions based on a condition.

- You use `else` and `else-if` within an `if` statement to extend the decision making beyond a single condition.

- Variables and constants belong to a certain scope, beyond which you cannot use them. A scope inherits variables and constants from its parent.

- You can use the ternary operator (a ? b : c) in place of simple `if` statements.

- You can use `switch` statements to decide which code to run depending on the value of a variable or constant.

- Enumerated types define a new type with a finite list of distinct values.

- `while` loops perform a certain task repeatedly as long as a condition is true.

- `do-while` loops always execute the loop at least once.

- The `break` statement lets you break out of a loop.

- `for` loops allow you to perform a loop a set number of times.

- The `continue` statement ends the current iteration of a loop and begins the next iteration.

Chapter 5: Functions

By Jonathan Sande

Each week, there are tasks that you repeat over and over: eat breakfast, brush your teeth, write your name, read books about Dart, and so on. Each of those tasks can be divided up into smaller tasks. Brushing your teeth, for example, includes putting toothpaste on the brush, brushing each tooth and rinsing your mouth out with water.

The same idea exists in computer programming. A **function** is one small task, or sometimes a collection of several smaller, related tasks that you can use in conjunction with other functions to accomplish a larger task.

In this chapter, you'll learn how to write functions in Dart, including both **named functions** and **anonymous functions**.

Function basics

You can think of functions like machines; they take something you provide to them (the input), and produce something different (the output).

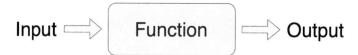

There are many examples of this in daily life. With an apple juicer, you put in apples and you get out apple juice. The input is apples; the output is juice. A dishwasher is another example. The input is dirty dishes, and the output is clean dishes. Blenders, coffee makers, microwaves and ovens are all like real-world functions that accept an input and produce an output.

Don't repeat yourself

Assume you have a small, useful piece of code that you've repeated in multiple places throughout your program:

```
// one place
if (fruit == 'banana') {
  peelBanana();
  eatBanana();
}

// another place
if (fruit == 'banana') {
  peelBanana();
  eatBanana();
}

// some other place
if (fruit == 'banana') {
  peelBanana();
  eatBanana();
}
```

Now, that code works rather well, but repeating that code in multiple spots presents at least two problems. The first problem is that you're duplicating effort by having this code in multiple places in your program. The second, and more troubling problem, is that if you need to change the logic in that bit of code later on, you'll have to track down all of those instances of the code and change them in the same way. That creates a high possibility that you'll make a mistake somewhere, or even miss changing one of the instances because you didn't see it.

Over time, this problem has led to some sound advice for writing clean code: **don't repeat yourself**, abbreviated as **DRY**. This term was originally coined in the book *The Pragmatic Programmer* by Andrew Hunt and David Thomas. Writing DRY code will help you prevent many bugs from creeping into your programs.

Functions are one of the main solutions to the duplication problem in the example above. Instead of repeating blocks of code in multiple places, you can simply package that code into a function and call that function from wherever you need to.

Anatomy of a Dart function

In Dart, a function consists of a return type, a name, a parameter list in parentheses and a body enclosed in braces.

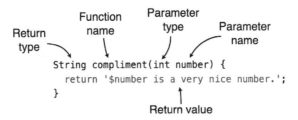

Here is a short summary of the labeled parts of the function:

- **Return type**: This comes first; it tells you immediately what the type will be of the function output. This particular function will return a `String`, but your functions can return any type you like. If the function won't return anything, that is, if it performs some work but doesn't produce an output value, you can use `void` as return type.

- **Function name**: You can name functions almost anything you like, but you should follow the `lowerCamelCase` naming convention. You'll learn a few more naming conventions a little later in this chapter.

- **Parameters**: Parameters are the input to the function; they go inside the parentheses after the function name. This example has only one parameter, but if you had more than one, you would separate them with commas. For each parameter, you write the type first, followed by the name. Just as with variable names, you should use `lowerCamelCase` for your parameter names.

- **Return value**: This is the function's output, and it should match the return type. In the example above, the function returns a `String` value by using the `return` keyword. If the return type is `void`, though, then you don't return anything.

The return type, function name and parameters are collectively known as the **function signature**. The code between the braces is known as the **function body**.

This is what the function above looks like in the context of a program:

```
void main() {
  const input = 12;
  final output = compliment(input);
  print(output);
}

String compliment(int number) {
  return '$number is a very nice number.';
}
```

What have we here? Not one function, but two? Yes, main is also a function, and one you've seen many times already. It's the function that every Dart program starts with. Since main doesn't return a value, the return type of main must be void. Although main can take parameters, there aren't any in this case, so there's only a pair of empty parentheses that follow the function name.

Notice that the compliment function is *outside* of main. Dart supports **top-level functions**, which are functions that aren't inside a class or another function. Conversely, you may nest one function inside another. And when a function is inside a class, it's called a **method**, which you'll learn more about in Chapter 6.

You call a function by writing its name, and providing the **argument**, which is the value you provide inside the parentheses as the parameter to the function. In this case, you're calling the compliment function and passing in an argument of 12. Run the code now and you'll see the following result:

```
12 is a very nice number.
```

Indeed, twelve *is* a nice number. It's the largest one-syllable number in English.

> **Note**: It's easy to get the words *parameter* and *argument* mixed up. A **parameter** is the name and type that you define as an input for your function. An **argument**, on the other hand, is the actual value that you pass in. A parameter is abstract, while an argument is concrete.

More about parameters

Parameters are incredibly flexible in Dart, so they deserve their own section.

Using multiple parameters

In a Dart function, you can use any number of parameters. If you have more than one parameter for your function, simply separate them with commas. Here's a function with two parameters:

```
void helloPersonAndPet(String person, String pet) {
  print('Hello, $person, and your furry friend, $pet!');
}
```

Parameters like the ones above are called **positional parameters**, because you have to supply the arguments in the same order that you defined the parameters when you wrote the function. If you call the function with the parameters in the wrong order, you'll get something obviously wrong:

```
helloPersonAndPet('Fluffy', 'Chris');
// Hello, Fluffy, and your furry friend, Chris!
```

Making parameters optional

The function above was very nice, but it was a little rigid. For example, try the following:

```
helloPersonAndPet();
```

If you don't have exactly the right number of parameters, the compiler will complain to you:

```
2 positional argument(s) expected, but 0 found.
```

You defined helloPersonAndPet to take two arguments, but in this case, you didn't pass in any. It would be nice if the code could detect this, and just say, "Hello, you two!" if no names are provided. Thankfully, it's possible to have optional parameters in a Dart function!

Imagine you want a function that takes a first name, a last name and a title, and returns a single string with the various pieces of the person's name strung together:

```
String fullName(String first, String last, String title) {
  return '$title $first $last';
}
```

The thing is, not everyone has a title, or wants to use their title, so your function needs to treat the title as optional. To indicate that a parameter is optional, you surround the parameter with square brackets and add a question mark after the type, like so:

```
String fullName(String first, String last, [String? title]) {
  if (title != null) {
    return '$title $first $last';
  } else {
    return '$first $last';
  }
}
```

Writing [String? title] makes title optional. If you don't pass in a value for title, then it will have the value of null, which means "no value". The updated code checks for null to decide how to format the return string.

Here are two examples to test it out:

```
print(fullName('Ray', 'Wenderlich'));
print(fullName('Albert', 'Einstein', 'Professor'));
```

Run that now and you'll see the following:

```
Ray Wenderlich
Professor Albert Einstein
```

The function correctly handles the optional title.

Note: Technically speaking, the question mark in String? is not written *after* the type; it's an integral part *of* the type, that is, the nullable String? type. More on this in Chapter 7.

Providing default values

In the example above, you saw that the default value for an optional parameter was null. This isn't always the best value for a default, though. That's why Dart also gives you the power to change the default value of any parameter in your function by using the assignment operator.

Take a look at this example:

```
bool withinTolerance(int value, [int min = 0, int max = 10]) {
  return min <= value && value <= max;
}
```

There are three parameters here, two of which are optional: min and max. If you don't specify a value for them, then min will be 0 and max will be 10.

Here are some specific examples to illustrate that:

```
withinTolerance(5)  // true
withinTolerance(15) // false
```

Since 5 is between 0 and 10, this evaluates to true; but since 15 is greater than the default max of 10, it evaluates to false.

If you want to specify values other than the defaults, you can do that as well:

```
withinTolerance(9, 7, 11) // true
```

Since 9 is between 7 and 11, the function returns true.

Look at that function call again: withinTolerance(9, 7, 11). Imagine that you're reading through your code for the first time in a month. What do those three numbers even mean? If you've got a good memory, you might recall that one of them is value, but which one? The first one? Or was it the second one? Or maybe it was the last one.

If that wasn't bad enough, the following function call also returns true:

```
withinTolerance(9, 7) // true
```

Since the function uses positional parameters, the provided arguments must follow the order you defined the parameters. That means value is 9, min is 7 and max has the default of 10. But who could ever remember that?

Of course you could just **Command+click** the function name on a Mac, or **Control+click** on a PC, to go to the definition and remind yourself of what the parameters meant. But the point is that this code is extremely hard to read. If only there were a better way!

Well, now that you mention it…

Naming parameters

Dart allows you to use **named parameters** to make the meaning of the parameters more clear in function calls.

To create a named parameter, you surround it with curly braces instead of square brackets. Here's the same function as above, but using named parameters instead:

```
bool withinTolerance(int value, {int min = 0, int max = 10}) {
  return min <= value && value <= max;
}
```

Note the following:

- `min` and `max` are surrounded by braces, which means you *must* use the parameter names when you provide their argument values to the function.

- Like square brackets, curly braces make the parameters inside optional. Since `value` isn't inside the braces, though, it's still required.

To provide an argument, you use the parameter name, followed by a colon and then the argument value. Here is how you call the function now:

```
withinTolerance(9, min: 7, max: 11) // true
```

That's a lot clearer, isn't it? The names `min` and `max` make it obvious where the tolerance limits are now.

An additional benefit of named parameters is that you don't have to use them in the exact order in which they were defined. These are both equivalent ways to call the function:

```
withinTolerance(9, min: 7, max: 11) // true
withinTolerance(9, max: 11, min: 7) // true
```

And since named parameters are optional, that means the following function calls are also valid:

```
withinTolerance(5)             // true
withinTolerance(15)            // false

withinTolerance(5, min: 7)    // false
withinTolerance(15, max: 20) // true
```

In the first two lines, since `min` is `0` and `max` is `10` by default, values of `5` and `15` evaluate to `true` and `false` respectively. In the last two lines, the `min` and `max` defaults were changed, which also changed the outcomes of the evaluations.

Making named parameters required

You might like to make `value` a named parameter as well. That way you could call the function like so:

```
withinTolerance(value: 9, min: 7, max: 11)
```

However, this brings up a problem. Named parameters are optional by default, but `value` can't be optional. If it were, someone might try to use your function like this:

```
withinTolerance()
```

Should that return `true` or `false`? It doesn't make sense to return anything if you don't give the function a value. This is just a bug waiting to happen.

What you want is to make `value` required instead of optional, while still keeping it as a named parameter. You can achieve this by including `value` inside the curly braces and adding the `required` keyword in front:

```
bool withinTolerance({
  required int value,
  int min = 0,
  int max = 10,
}) {
  return min <= value && value <= max;
}
```

Since the function signature was getting a little long, adding a comma after the last parameter lets the IDE format it vertically. You still remember how to auto-format in VS Code, right? That's **Shift+Option+F** on a Mac or **Shift+Alt+F** on a PC.

With the `required` keyword in place, VS Code will warn you if you don't provide a value for `value` when you call the function:

```
bool withinTolerance({required int value, int min = 0, int max
= 10})

The named parameter 'value' is required, but there's no
corresponding argument.
Try adding the required
argument. dart(missing_required_argument)

View Problem (⌥F8)   Quick Fix... (⌘.)
print(withinTolerance());
```

Using named parameters makes your code more readable and is an important part of writing clean code when you have multiple inputs to a function. In the next section, you'll learn some more best practices for writing good functions.

Writing good functions

People have been writing code for decades. Along the way, they've designed some good practices to improve code quality and prevent errors. One of those practices is writing DRY code as you saw earlier. Here are a few more things to pay attention to as you learn about writing good functions.

Avoiding side effects

When you take medicine to cure a medical problem, but that medicine makes you fat, that's known as a side effect. If you put some bread in a toaster to make toast, but the toaster burns your house down, that's also a side effect. Not all side effects are bad, though. If you take a business trip to Paris, you also get to see the Eiffel Tower. *Magnifique!*

When you write a function, you know what the inputs are: the parameters. You also know what the output is: the return value. Anything beyond that, that is, anything that affects the world outside of the function, is a side effect.

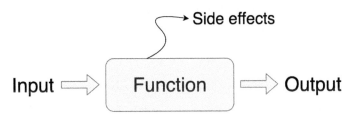

Have a look at this function:

```
void hello() {
  print('Hello!');
}
```

Printing something to the console is a side effect, because it's affecting the world outside of the function. If you wanted to rewrite your function so that there were no side effects, you could write it like this:

```
String hello() {
  return 'Hello!';
}
```

Now, there's nothing inside the function body that affects the outside world. You'll have to write the string to the console somewhere outside of the function.

It's fine, and even necessary, for some functions to have side effects. But as a general rule, functions without side effects are easier to deal with and reason about. You can rely on them to do exactly what you expect because they always return the same output for any given input. These kinds of functions are also called **pure functions**.

Here is another function with side effects to further illustrate the point:

```
var myPreciousData = 5782;

String anInnocentLookingFunction(String name) {
  myPreciousData = -1;
  return 'Hello, $name. Heh, heh, heh.';
}
```

Unless you took the time to study the code inside of anInnocentLookingFunction, you'd have no idea that calling this innocent-looking function would also change your precious data. That's because the function had an unknown side effect. This is also a good reminder about the dangers of using global variables like myPreciousData, as you never know who might change it.

Make it your ambition to maximize your use of pure functions, and minimize your use of functions with side effects.

Doing only one thing

Proponents of "clean code" recommend keeping your functions small and logically coherent. *Small* here means only a handful of lines of code. If a function is too big, or contains unrelated parts, consider breaking it into smaller functions.

Write your functions so that each one has only a single job to do. If you find yourself adding comments to describe different sections of a complex function, that's usually a good clue that you should break your function up into smaller functions. In clean coding, this is known as the **Single Responsibility Principle**. In addition to functions, this principle also applies to classes and libraries. But that's a topic for another chapter.

Choosing good names

You should always give your functions names that describe exactly what they do. If your code sounds like well-written prose, it'll be faster to read and easier to understand.

This naming advice applies to almost every programming language. However, there are a few additional naming conventions that Dart programmers like to follow. These are recommendations, not requirements, but keep them in mind as you code:

- Use noun phrases for pure functions; that is, ones without side effects. For example, use `averageTemperature` instead of `getAverageTemperature` and `studentNames` instead of `extractStudentNames`.

- Use verb phrases for functions with side effects. For example, `updateDatabase` or `printHello`.

- Also use verb phases if you want to emphasize that the function does a lot of work. For example, `calculateFibonacci` or `parseJson`.

- Don't repeat parameter names in the function name. For example, use `cube(int number)` instead of `cubeNumber(int number)`, or `printStudent(String name)` instead of `printStudentName(String name)`.

Optional types

Earlier you saw this function:

```
String compliment(int number) {
  return '$number is a very nice number.';
}
```

The return type is `String`, and the parameter type is `int`. Dart is an optionally-typed language, so it's possible to omit the types from your function declaration. In that case, the function would look like this:

```
compliment(number) {
  return '$number is a very nice number.';
}
```

Dart can infer that the return type here is `String`, but it has to fall back on `dynamic` for the unknown parameter type. The following function is the equivalent of what Dart sees:

```
String compliment(dynamic number) {
  return '$number is a very nice number.';
}
```

While it's permissible to omit return and parameter types, this book recommends that you include them at the very least for situations where Dart can't infer the type. As you learned in Chapter 3, there's a much greater advantage to writing Dart in a statically-typed way.

Mini-exercises

1. Write a function named `youAreWonderful`, with a String parameter called `name`. It should return a string using `name`, and say something like "You're wonderful, Bob."

2. Add another `int` parameter to that function called `numberPeople` so that the function returns something like "You're wonderful, Bob. 10 people think so."

3. Make both inputs named parameters. Make `name` required and set `numberPeople` to have a default of `30`.

Anonymous functions

All the functions you've seen previously in this chapter, such as `main`, `hello`, and `withinTolerance` are **named** functions, which means, well, they have a name.

```
            Function
             name
                \
String compliment(int number) {
  return '$number is a very nice number.';
}
```

But not every function needs a name. If you remove the return type and the function name, then what you have left is an anonymous function:

```
~~String compliment~~(int number) {
  return '$number is a very nice number.';
}
```

The return type will be inferred from the return value of the function body, `String` in this case.

So, why all the stealth by being anonymous, you ask? Are functions concerned about their online privacy, too? Well, that's not quite it. Sometimes you only need functions in one specific spot in your code, for one specific reason, and there's no reason to give that function a name. You'll see some examples of this soon.

First-class citizens

In Dart, functions are **first-class citizens**. That means you can treat them like any other other type, assigning functions as values to variables and even passing functions around as parameters or returning them from other functions.

Assigning functions to variables

When assigning a value to a variable, functions behave just like other types:

```
int number = 4;
String greeting = 'hello';
bool isHungry = true;
```

```
Function multiply = (int a, int b) {
  return a * b;
};
```

The type of multiply is Function, the same way that number is int, greeting is String and isHungry is bool. On the right hand side of each assignment, you have literal values: 4 is an integer literal, 'hello' is a string literal, true is a Boolean literal, and the anonymous function you see above is a function literal.

One reason that you need anonymous functions is that you can't assign a named function to a variable:

```
Function myFunction = int multiply(int a, int b) {
  return a * b;
};
```

Trying to do that produces the following error:

```
Function expressions can't be named.
```

Passing functions to functions

Just as you can write a function to take int or String as a parameter, you can also have Function as a parameter:

```
void namedFunction(Function anonymousFunction) {
  // function body
}
```

Here, namedFunction takes an anonymous function as a parameter.

Returning functions from functions

Just as you can pass in functions as input parameters, you can also return them as output:

```
Function namedFunction() {
  return () {
    print('hello');
  };
}
```

The return value is an anonymous function of type Function.

Functions that return functions, or that accept them as parameters, are called **higher order functions**.

Using anonymous functions

Now that you know where you can use anonymous functions, try a hand at doing it yourself. Take the multiply function again:

```
final multiply = (int a, int b) {
  return a * b;
};
```

To call the function that the variable multiply refers to, simply use the variable name followed by the arguments in parentheses:

```
print(multiply(2, 3));
```

This will print 6 just as if you were calling the named function multiply.

Returning a function

Have a look at a different example:

```
Function applyMultiplier(num multiplier) {
  return (num value) {
    return value * multiplier;
  };
}
```

This one looks a little crazy at first. There are two return statements! To make sense of a function like this, look at it this way: applyMultiplier is a named function that returns an anonymous function. It's like a machine that makes a machine. That second return statement belongs to the anonymous function and won't get called when applyMultiplier is called.

Now write the following line:

```
final triple = applyMultiplier(3);
```

triple is a constant variable of type Function; that is, the anonymous function that applyMultiplier returned. You haven't run that anonymous function yet. You're simply storing it in a variable named triple.

Run it now:

```
print(triple(6));
print(triple(14.0));
```

Passing arguments to the variable runs the function. Because the parameter type was num, it can accept both int and double inputs. This is the result:

```
18
42.0
```

Going back to the machine-that-makes-a-machine analogy, passing 3 into applyMultiplier was like setting a dial on the first machine. You set it to "make tripling machines." So what you got out was a machine that triples everything you give it. If you had set the dial on the first machine to 4, then you would have gotten quadrupling machines, if 2, then doubling machines.

Anonymous functions in forEach loops

Chapter 4 introduced you to forEach loops, which iterate over a collection. Although you may not have realized it, that was an example of using an anonymous function.

So if you have a list of numbers, like so:

```
const numbers = [1, 2, 3];
```

You can call forEach on the list and pass in an anonymous function that triples each number in the list and prints out that value.

```
numbers.forEach((number) {
  final tripled = number * 3;
  print(tripled);
});
```

The parameter type of number is inferred from the list element types; in this case, int. Run the code and you'll see the following result:

```
3
6
9
```

Earlier in this chapter you learned how functions are a way to package reusable code that you can call in multiple places. The example here shows one of the main benefits of anonymous functions, which is packaging up logic that you *don't* need in multiple places, so you don't need to make it a named function. You simply need to pass the logic around either as input to, or as output from, another function.

Closures and scope

Anonymous functions in Dart act as what are known as **closures**. The term closure means that the code "closes around" the surrounding scope, and therefore has access to variables and functions defined within that scope.

```
                          {
                            var age = 42;
                            (parameters) {  ◄────────  another scope
         a scope              // have access to age
                              age = 43;
                            }  ◄───────────
                          }
```

A scope in Dart is defined by a pair of curly braces. All the code within these braces is a scope. You can even have nested scopes within other scopes. Examples of scopes are function bodies and the bodies of loops.

The return value of the applyMultiplier function from before is an example of a closure.

```
Function applyMultiplier(num multiplier) {
  return (num value) {
    return value * multiplier;
  };
}
```

The anonymous function it returns closes over the multiplier value that's passed in as a parameter to applyMultiplier.

As another example, if you have a variable counter and then define an anonymous function below it, that anonymous function acts like a closure and has access to counter, and so can change it.

```
var counter = 0;
final incrementCounter = () {
  counter += 1;
};
```

The anonymous function that defines incrementCounter can access counter, even though counter is not a parameter to the anonymous function, nor is it defined in the function body.

Call `incrementCounter` five times and print `counter`:

```
incrementCounter();
incrementCounter();
incrementCounter();
incrementCounter();
incrementCounter();
print(counter); // 5
```

You'll see that `counter` now has a value of 5.

You can use a closure as a function return value, and, as in this example, count the number of times a given function has been called.

```
Function countingFunction() {
  var counter = 0;
  final incrementCounter = () {
    counter += 1;
    return counter;
  };
  return incrementCounter;
}
```

Each function returned by `countingFunction` will have its own version of `counter`. So if you were to generate two functions with `countingFunction`, like so:

```
final counter1 = countingFunction();
final counter2 = countingFunction();
```

...then each call to those functions will increment its own `counter` independently:

```
print(counter1()); // 1
print(counter2()); // 1
print(counter1()); // 2
print(counter1()); // 3
print(counter2()); // 2
```

Mini-exercises

1. Change the `youAreWonderful` function in the first mini-exercise of this chapter into an anonymous function. Assign it to a variable called `wonderful`.

2. Using `forEach`, print a message telling the people in the following list that they're wonderful.

```
const people = ['Chris', 'Tiffani', 'Pablo'];
```

Arrow functions

Dart has a special syntax for functions whose body is only one line. Consider the following named function add that adds two numbers together:

```dart
int add(int a, int b) {
  return a + b;
}
```

Since the body is only one line, you can convert it to the following form:

```dart
int add(int a, int b) => a + b;
```

You replaced the function's braces and body with an arrow (=>) and left off the return keyword. The return value is whatever the value of the expression is. Writing a function in this way is known as **arrow syntax** or **arrow notation**.

You can also use arrow syntax with anonymous functions. You're simply left with the parameter list, the arrow, and a single expression:

```dart
(parameters) => expression;
```

In the following examples, you're going to **refactor**, or rewrite, some of the anonymous functions you saw earlier in the chapter.

Refactoring example 1

The body of the anonymous function you assigned to multiply has one line:

```dart
final multiply = (int a, int b) {
  return a * b;
};
```

You can convert it to use arrow syntax as follows:

```dart
final multiply = (int a, int b) => a * b;
```

You can call it just as you did before, with the same result:

```dart
print(multiply(2, 3)); // 6
```

Refactoring example 2

You can also use arrow syntax for the anonymous function returned by
`applyMultiplier`:

```
Function applyMultiplier(num multiplier) {
  return (num value) {
    return value * multiplier;
  };
}
```

With arrow syntax, the function becomes:

```
Function applyMultiplier(num multiplier) {
  return (num value) => value * multiplier;
}
```

The result of the function is the same as before.

Refactoring example 3

You can't use arrow syntax on the `forEach` example, though:

```
numbers.forEach((number) {
  final tripled = number * 3;
  print(tripled);
});
```

That's because there's more than one line in the function body. However, if you
rewrote it to fit on line, that would work:

```
numbers.forEach((number) => print(number * 3));
```

Mini-exercise

Change the `forEach` loop in the previous "You're wonderful" mini-exercise to use
arrow syntax.

Challenges

Before moving on, here are some challenges to test your knowledge of functions. It's best if you try to solve them yourself, but solutions are available in the **challenge** folder for this chapter if you get stuck.

Challenge 1: Prime time

Write a function that checks if a number is prime.

Challenge 2: Can you repeat that?

Write a function named repeatTask with the following definition:

```
int repeatTask(int times, int input, Function task)
```

It repeats a given task on input for times number of times.

Pass an anonymous function to repeatTask to square the input of 2 four times. Confirm that you get the result 65536, since 2 squared is 4, 4 squared is 16, 16 squared is 256, and 256 squared is 65536.

Challenge 3: Darts and arrows

Update Challenge 2 to use arrow syntax.

Key points

- Functions package related blocks of code into reusable units.

- A function signature includes the return type, name and parameters. The function body is the code between the braces.

- Parameters can be positional or named, and required or optional.

- Side effects are anything, besides the return value, that change the world outside of the function body.

- To write clean code, use functions that are short and only do one thing.

- Anonymous functions don't have a function name, and the return type is inferred.

- Dart functions are first-class citizens and thus can be assigned to variables and passed around as values.

- Anonymous functions act as closures, capturing any variables or functions within its scope.

- Arrow syntax is a shorthand way to write one-line functions.

Where to go from here?

This chapter spoke briefly about the Single Responsibility Principle and other clean coding principles. Do a search for **SOLID principles** to learn even more. It'll be time well spent.

Some aspects of Dart are hard-and-fast rules. Other aspects, like how to name variables and functions, are common practices, and while not required, they do make it easier to read the code and share it with others. Improve your understanding of these conventions by reading **Effective Dart** in the dart.dev guides.

You've heard briefly about methods and classes; you'll explore these ideas more in the next chapter.

Chapter 6: Classes

By Jonathan Sande

So far in this book, you've used built-in types such as `int`, `String` and `bool`. You've also seen one way to make custom types using enum. In this chapter, you'll learn a more flexible way to create your own types by using **classes**.

> **Note**: Because there's quite a bit to learn about classes and object-oriented programming, or OOP, in Dart, you'll come back to the subject again in Chapter 9. In that chapter, you'll learn how to create a hierarchy of classes using inheritance as well as some other advanced topics. Don't be afraid of the word "advanced," though. You can handle it. It'll only be more advanced than this chapter is. If you have experience with any other OOP languages, you probably know most of it already anyway.

Dart classes

Classes are like architectural blueprints that tell the system how to make an **object**, where an object is the actual data that's stored in the computer's memory. If a class is the blueprint, then you could say the object is like the house that the blueprint represents. For example, the String class describes its data as a collection of UTF-16 code units, but a String object is something concrete like 'Hello, Dart!'.

All values in Dart are objects that are built from a class. This includes the values of basic types like int, double and bool. That's different from other languages like Java, where basic types are primitive. For example, if you have x = 10 in Java, the value of x is 10 itself. However, Dart doesn't have primitive types. Even for a simple int, the value is an object that wraps the integer. You'll learn more on this concept later.

Classes are a core component of object-oriented programming. They're used to combine data *and* functions inside a single structure.

```
class MyClass {
  var myProperty = 'Hello, Dart!';    ◄─────── data

  // constructor
  MyClass();    ◄─────────

  void myMethod() {    ◄─────────    functions
    print(myProperty);
  }
}
```

The functions exist to transform the data. Functions inside of a class are known as **methods**, while **constructors** are special methods you use to create objects from the class.

It's time to get your hands dirty. Working with classes is far more instructive than reading about them!

Defining a class

To get started creating your own types, you'll make a simple User class that has id and name properties. This is just the kind of class that you're highly likely to create in the future for an app that requires users to log in.

Write the following simple class at the top level of your Dart file. Your class should be outside of the main function, either above or below it.

```
class User {
  int id = 0;
  String name = '';
}
```

This creates a class named User. It has two properties; id is an int with a default value of 0, and name is a String with the default value of an empty string.

> **Note**: Depending on the situation, null may be a better default than 0 or ''. However, since nullable types and null safety won't be fully covered until Chapter 7, this chapter will simply use reasonable defaults for properties.

Creating an object from a class

As mentioned above, the value you create from a class is called an object. Another name for an object is **instance**, so creating an object is sometimes called **instantiating a class**.

Since coding the class in your Dart file as you did above simply creates the blueprint, a User object doesn't exist yet. You can create one by calling the class name as you would call a function. Add the following line inside the main function:

```
final user = User();
```

This creates an instance of your User class and stores that instance, or object, in user. Notice the empty parentheses after User. It looks like you're calling a function without any parameters. In fact, you are calling a type of function called a **constructor method**. You'll learn a lot more about them later in the chapter. Right now, simply understand that using your class in this way creates an instance of your class.

The optional keyword new

Before version 2.0 of Dart came out, you had to use the new keyword to create an object from a class. At that time, creating a new instance of a class would have looked like this:

```
final user = new User();
```

In fact, this still works, but the new keyword is completely optional now, so it's better to just leave it off. Why clutter your code with unnecessary words, right?

You'll still come across new from time to time in the documentation or in legacy code, but at least now you won't be confused by it. You can delete it if you come across it.

Assigning values to properties

Now that you have an instance of User stored in user, you can assign new values to this object's properties by using **dot notation**. To access the name property, type user *dot* name, and then give it a value:

```
user.name = 'Ray';
```

Now, set the ID in a similar way:

```
user.id = 42;
```

Your code should look like the following:

```
void main() {
  final user = User();
  user.name = 'Ray';
  user.id = 42;
}

class User {
  int id = 0;
  String name = '';
}
```

You'll notice that you have both a function and a class together. Dart allows you to put multiple classes, top-level functions and even top-level variables all together in the same file. Their order in the file isn't important. User is located below main here, but if you put it above main, that's fine as well.

You've defined a User data type with a class, created an object from it and assigned values to its parameters. Run the code now, though, and you won't see anything special happen. The next section will show you how to display data from an object.

Printing an object

You can print any object in Dart. However, if you try to print `user` now, you won't get quite what you hoped for. Add the following line at the bottom of the `main` function and run the code:

```
print(user);
```

Here's what you get:

```
Instance of 'User'
```

Hmm, you were likely expecting something about Ray and the ID. What gives?

All classes in Dart (well, except for `Null`, but that's a topic for Chapter 7) are derived from `Object`, which has a `toString` method. In this case, your object doesn't tell Dart how to write its internal data when you call `toString` on it, so Dart gives you this generic, default output instead. However, you can override the `Object` class's version of `toString` by writing your own implementation of `toString`, and thus customize how your own object will print out.

Add the following method to the `User` class:

```
@override
String toString() {
  return 'User(id: $id, name: $name)';
}
```

Words that start with @ are called **annotations**. Including them is optional and doesn't change how the code executes. However, annotations *do* give the compiler more information so that it can help you out at compile time. Here, the `@override` annotation is telling both you and the compiler that `toString` is a method in `Object` that you want to override with your own customized version, so if you accidentally wrote the `toString` method signature incorrectly, the compiler would warn you about it because of the `@override` annotation.

Since methods have access to the class properties, you simply use that data to output a more meaningful message when someone prints your object. Run the code now, and you'll see the following result:

```
User(id: 42, name: Ray)
```

That's far more useful!

> **Note**: Your User class only has a single method right now, but in classes with many methods, most programmers put the toString method at or near the bottom of the class instead of burying it in the middle somewhere. As you continue to add to User, keep toString at the bottom. Following conventions like this makes navigating and reading the code easier.

Adding methods

Now that you've learned to override methods, you're going to move on and add your own methods to the User class. But before you do, there's a little background information that you should know.

Understanding object serialization

Being able to organize related data into a class is super useful, especially when you want to pass that data around as a unit within your app. One disadvantage, though, shows up when you're saving the object or sending it over the network. Files, databases and networks only know how to handle simple data types, such as numbers and strings. They don't know how to handle anything more complex, like your User data type.

Serialization is the process of converting a complex data object into a string. Once the object has been serialized, it's easy to save that data or transfer it across the network because everything from your app to the network and beyond knows how to deal with strings. Later, when you want to read that data back in, you can do so by way of **deserialization**, which is simply the process of converting a string back into an object of your data type.

You didn't realize it, but you actually serialized your User object in the toString method above. The code you wrote was good enough to get the job done, but you didn't really follow any standardized format. You simply wrote it out in a way that looked nice to the human eye. If you gave that string to someone else, though, they might have some difficulty understanding how to deserialize it, that is, convert it back into a User object.

It turns out that serialization and deserialization are such common tasks that people have devised a number of standardized formats for serializing data. One of the most common is called **JSON**: JavaScript Object Notation. Despite the name, it's used far and wide outside the world of JavaScript.

JSON isn't difficult to learn, but this chapter will only show you enough JSON to serialize your User object into a more portable format. Check the *Where to go from here* section at the end of the chapter to find out where you can learn more about this format.

Adding a JSON serialization method

You're going to add another method to your class now that will convert a User object to JSON format. It'll be similar to what you did in toString.

Add the following method to the User class, putting it above the toString method:

```
String toJson() {
  return '{"id":$id,"name":"$name"}';
}
```

Here are a few things to note:

- Since this is your own custom method and you're not overriding a method that belongs to another class, you don't add the @override annotation.

- In Dart naming conventions, acronyms are treated as words. Thus, toJson is a better name than toJSON.

- There's nothing magic about serialization in this case. You simply used string interpolation to insert the property values in the correct locations in the JSON formatted string.

- In JSON, objects are surrounded by curly braces, properties are separated by commas, property names are separated from property values by colons, and strings are surrounded by double-quotes. If a string needs to include a double-quote inside itself, you escape it with a backslash like so: \"

- JSON is very similar to a Dart data type called Map. In fact, Dart even has built-in functions in the dart:convert library to serialize and deserialize JSON maps. And that's actually what most people use to serialize objects. However, you haven't read Chapter 8 about maps yet, so this example is going to be low-tech. You'll see a little preview of Map, though, in the fromJson example later in this chapter.

To test out your new function, add the following line to the bottom of the main method:

```
print(user.toJson());
```

This code calls the custom toJson method on your user object using dot notation.

The dot goes between the object name and method name just like you saw earlier for accessing a property name.

Run the code and you'll see the following:

```
{"id":42,"name":"Ray"}
```

It's very similar to what toString gave you, but this time it's in standard JSON format, so a computer on the other side of the world could easily convert that back into a Dart object.

Cascade notation

When you created your User object above, you set its parameters like so:

```
final user = User();
user.name = 'Ray';
user.id = 42;
```

However, Dart offers a cascade operator (..) that allows you to chain together multiple assignments on the same object without having to repeat the object name. The following code is equivalent:

```
final user = User()
  ..name = 'Ray'
  ..id = 42;
```

Note that the semicolon only appears on the last line.

Cascade notation isn't strictly necessary, but it does makes your code just a little tidier when you have to assign a long list of properties or repeatedly call a method that modifies your object.

Mini-exercises

1. Create a class called Password and give it a string property called value.

2. Override the toString method of Password so that it prints value.

3. Add a method to Password called isValid that returns true only if the length of value is greater than 8.

Constructors

Constructors are methods that create, or *construct*, instances of a class. That is to say, constructors build new objects. Constructors have the same name as the class, and the implicit return type of the constructor method is also the same type as the class itself.

Default constructor

As it stands, your User class doesn't have an explicit constructor. In cases like this, Dart provides a default constructor that takes no parameters and just returns an instance of the class. For example, defining a class like this:

```
class Address {
  var value = '';
}
```

Is equivalent to writing it like this:

```
class Address {
  Address();
  var value = '';
}
```

Including the default Address() constructor is optional.

Sometimes you don't want the default constructor, though. You'd like to initialize the data in an object at the same time that you create the object. The next section shows how to do just that.

Custom constructors

If you want to pass parameters to the constructor to modify how your class builds an object, you can. It's similar to how you wrote functions with parameters in Chapter 5.

Like the default constructor above, the constructor name should be the same as the class name. This type of constructor is called a **generative constructor** because it directly generates an object of the same type.

Long-form constructor

In Dart the convention is to put the constructor before the property variables. Add the following generative constructor method at the top of the class body:

```dart
User(int id, String name) {
  this.id = id;
  this.name = name;
}
```

This is known as a **long-form constructor**. You'll understand why it's considered "long-form" when you see the short-form constructor later.

This is what the class looks like (without the toJson and toString methods):

```dart
class User {
  User(int id, String name) {
    this.id = id;
    this.name = name;
  }

  int id = 0;
  String name = '';

  // ...
}
```

this is a new keyword. What does it do?

The keyword this in the constructor body allows you to disambiguate which variable you're talking about. It means *this* object. So this.name refers the object property called name, while name (without this) refers to the constructor parameter. Using the same name for the constructor parameters as the class properties is called **shadowing**. So the constructor above takes the id and name parameters and uses this to initialize the properties of the object.

Delete everything from inside the main function body. Then add the following code in its place to create a User object by passing in some arguments:

```dart
final user = User(42, 'Ray');
print(user);
```

Once the object has been created, you can access its properties and other methods just as you did before. However, you can't use the default constructor User() anymore, since id and name are required positional parameters.

Short-form constructor

Dart also has a **short-form constructor** where you don't provide a function body, but you instead list the properties you want to initialize, prefixed with the `this` keyword. Arguments you send to the short form constructor are used to initialize the corresponding object properties.

Here is the long form constructor that you currently have:

```
User(int id, String name) {
  this.id = id;
  this.name = name;
}
```

Now replace that with the following short-form constructor:

```
User(this.id, this.name);
```

Dart infers the constructor parameter types of `int` and `String` from the properties themselves that are declared in the class body.

The class should now look like this:

```
class User {
  User(this.id, this.name);

  int id = 0;
  String name = '';

  // ...
}
```

Run the code again. You'll see the short-form constructor works just like the longer form you replaced, but it's just a little tidier now.

> **Note**: You could remove the default property values of `0` and `' '` at this point since `id` and `name` are guaranteed to be initialized by the constructor parameters. However, there's an intermediate step in the next section where they'll still be useful. Keeping the default values a little longer will allow this chapter to postpone dealing with null safety until it can be covered more fully in Chapter 7.

Named constructors

Dart also has a second type of generative constructor called a **named constructor**, which you create by adding an identifier on to the class name. It takes the following pattern:

```
ClassName.identifierName()
```

From here on, this chapter will refer to a constructor without the identifier, that is, one which only uses the class name, as an **unnamed constructor**.

Why would you want a named constructor instead of the nice, tidy default one? Well, sometimes you have some common cases that you want to provide a convenience constructor for. Or maybe you have some special edge cases for constructing certain classes that need a slightly different approach.

Say, for example, that you want to have an anonymous user with a preset ID and name. You can do that by creating a named constructor. Add the following named constructor below the short-form constructor:

```
User.anonymous() {
  id = 0;
  name = 'anonymous';
}
```

The identifier, or named part, of the constructor is .anonymous. Named constructors may have parameters, but in this case, there are none. And since there aren't any parameter names to get confused with, you don't need to use this.id or this.name. Rather, you just use the property variables id and name directly.

Call the named constructor in main like so:

```
final anonymousUser = User.anonymous();
print(anonymousUser);
```

Run that and you'll see the expected output:

```
User(id: 0, name: anonymous)
```

> **Note**: Without default values for `id` and `name`, Dart would have complained that these variables weren't being initialized, even though `User.anonymous` does in fact initialize them in the constructor body. You could solve the problem by using the `late` keyword, but that's a topic for Chapter 7 — hence the default values here.

Forwarding constructors

In the named constructor example above, you set the class properties directly in the constructor body. However, this doesn't follow the DRY principle you learned earlier. You're repeating yourself by having two different locations where you can set the properties. It's not a huge deal, but imagine that you have five different constructors instead of two. It would be easy to forget to update all five if you had to make a change, and if the constructor logic were complicated, it would be easy to make a mistake.

One way to solve this issue is by calling the main constructor from the named constructor. This is called **forwarding** or **redirecting**. To do that, you use the keyword `this` again.

Delete the `anonymous` named constructor that you created above and replace it with the following:

```
User.anonymous() : this(0, 'anonymous');
```

This time there's no constructor body, but instead, you follow the name with a colon and then forward the properties on to the unnamed constructor. The forwarding syntax replaces `User` with `this`.

Also, now that you've moved property initialization from the constructor body to the parameter list, Dart is finally convinced that `id` and `name` are guaranteed to be initialized. Replace these two lines:

```
int id = 0;
String name = '';
```

with the following:

```
int id;
String name;
```

No complaints from Dart.

You call the named constructor exactly like you did before:

```
final anonymousUser = User.anonymous();
```

The results are the same as well.

Optional and named parameters

Everything you learned about function parameters in Chapter 5 also applies to constructor method parameters. That means you can make parameters optional using square brackets:

```
MyClass([this.myProperty]);
```

Or you can make them optional and named using curly braces:

```
MyClass({this.myProperty});
```

Or named and required using curly braces and the `required` keyword:

```
MyClass({required this.myProperty});
```

Adding named parameters for User

Earlier when you instantiated a `User` object, you did this:

```
final user = User(42, 'Ray');
```

For someone not familiar with your `User` class, they might think 42 is Ray's age, or his password, or how many pet cats he has. Using named parameters here would help a lot with readability.

Refactor the unnamed constructor in `User` by adding braces around the parameters. Since that makes the parameters optional, you could use the `required` keyword as you saw in Chapter 5, but this time simply give them default values:

```
User({this.id = 0, this.name = 'anonymous'});
```

The compiler will complain at this, because that change also requires refactoring the anonymous named constructor to use the parameter names in the redirect.

However, since the parameter defaults are now just what the anonymous constructor was doing before, you can delete the anonymous constructor and replace it with the following:

```
User.anonymous() : this();
```

Using the named constructor will now forward to the unnamed constructor with no arguments.

In `main`, the way to create an anonymous user is still the same, but now the way to create Ray's user object is like so:

```
final user = User(id: 42, name: 'Ray');
```

That's a lot more readable. They're not cats; it's clearly just an ID.

In case you've gotten lost, here's what things look like now:

```
class User {
  // unnamed constructor
  User({this.id = 0, this.name = 'anonymous'});

  // named constructor
  User.anonymous() : this();

  int id;
  String name;

  // ...
}
```

Initializer lists

You might have discovered a small problem that exists with your class as it's now written. Take a look at the following way that an unscrupulous person could use this class:

```
final vicki = User(id: 24, name: 'Vicki');
vicki.name = 'Nefarious Hacker';
print(vicki);
// User(id: 24, name: Nefarious Hacker)
```

If those statements were spread throughout the code base instead of being in one place as they are here, someone printing the `vicki` user object and expecting a real name would get a surprise. "Nefarious Hacker" is definitely not what you'd expect. Once you've created the `User` object, you don't want anyone to mess with it.

But forget nefarious hackers; *you're* the one who's most likely to change a property and then forget you did it.

There are a couple of ways to solve this problem. You'll see one solution now and a fuller solution later.

Private variables

Dart allows you to make variables private by adding an underscore (_) in front of their name.

Change the id property to _id and name to _name. Since these variables are used in several locations throughout your code, let VS Code help you out. Put your cursor on the variable name and press F2. Edit the variable name and press **Enter** to change all of the references at once.

```
class User {
  User({this.id = 0, this.name = 'anonymous'});

  User.anonymous() : this();

  int id;
  Stri _id
       Enter to Rename, ⇧Enter to Preview
  String toJson() {
    return '{"id":$id,"name":"$name"}';
  }
```

Oh…, that actually renamed a few more things than you intended since it also renamed what was in the main function. But that's OK. Just delete everything inside the body of main for now.

There is still one problem left with the unnamed constructor in User:

```
User({this._id = 0, this._name = 'anonymous'});
```

The compiler gives you an error:

```
Named parameters can't start with an underscore.
```

Fix that by deleting the unnamed constructor and replacing it with the following:

```
User({int id = 0, String name = 'anonymous'})
      : _id = id,
        _name = name;
```

Do you see the colon that precedes _id? The comma-separated list that comes after it is called the **initializer list**. One use for this list is exactly what you've done here. Externally, the parameters have one name, while internally, you're using private variable names.

The initializer list is always executed before the body of the constructor, if the body exists. You don't need a body for this constructor, but if you wanted to add one, it would look like this:

```
User({int id = 0, String name = 'anonymous'})
      : _id = id,
        _name = name {
   print('User name is $_name');
}
```

The constructor would initialize _id and _name before it ran the print statement inside the braces.

> **Note:** The member variables of a class are generally called **fields**. However, when the fields are public, that is, when they're visible to the outside world, you can also call them **properties**. The Getters and Setters sections below will show you how to use public properties and private fields at the same time.

Why aren't the private properties private?

It turns out that your nefarious hacker can still access the "private" fields of User. Add the following two lines to main to see this in action:

```
final vicki = User(id: 24, name: 'Vicki');
vicki._name = 'Nefarious Hacker';
```

What's that all about? Well, using an underscore before a variable or method name makes it **library private**, not **class private**. For your purposes in this chapter, a library is simply a file. Since the main function and the User class are in the same file, nothing in User is hidden from main. To see private variables in action, you'll need to make another file so that you aren't using your class in the same file in which it's defined.

Create a new file called **user.dart** in the same folder as the file you've been working with. In VS Code, you can click on the current file in the Explorer panel and then press the **New File button**.

Now move the entire User class over to **user.dart**.

Back in the previous file with the main function (if you're using the starter project, it would be named starter.dart), add the library import to the top of the class like so:

```
import 'user.dart';
```

Now you'll notice that in the main function you no longer have access to _name:

```
vicki._name = 'Nefarious Hacker';
```

This produces an error:

```
The setter '_name' isn't defined for the type 'User'.
```

Great! Now it's no longer possible to change the properties after the object has been created. Delete or comment out that entire line:

```
// vicki._name = 'Nefarious Hacker';
```

Before leaving this section on initializer lists, there's one more thing to talk about: errors.

Checking for errors

Initializer lists are a great place to check for errors in the constructor parameters, which you can do by adding assert statements. Think of asserts like sanity checks that make sure you aren't doing anything silly, by checking that a condition is in fact true.

An assert statement takes a condition, and if the condition is false, terminates the app. This only happens during debugging, though. The compiler completely ignores assert statements in release builds.

Replace the unnamed constructor with the following updated version:

```
User({int id = 0, String name = 'anonymous'})
    : assert(id >= 0),
      assert(name.isNotEmpty),
      _id = id,
      _name = name;
```

Note the two `assert` statements in the initializer list; it's customary to put these asserts at the top of the list. The first assert checks that `id` is greater than or equal to zero, and the second one checks that `name` actually has a value. Of course you don't want a negative ID or an empty name. If either of those conditions ever occurs, then terminating is your best bet, as it gives you a loud and clear message that you need to handle that situation in code before a `User` is ever created.

Add the following line to the bottom of the `main` function:

```
final jb = User(id: -1, name: 'JB Lorenzo');
```

Run the project and you'll get an error:

```
Failed assertion: line 3 pos 16: 'id >= 0': is not true.
```

Note: If you're running Dart from the command line rather than from VS Code, you won't get `assert` errors unless you enable them with the --enable-asserts flag. Assuming your `main` function is in a file called **starter.dart**, you should run your program in this way:

```
dart --enable-asserts starter.dart
```

Since `id` must be greater than or equal to zero, either comment out the line or change `id` to a positive number.

```
// final jb = User(id: 100, name: 'JB Lorenzo');
```

Constant constructors

You've already learned how to keep people from modifying the properties of a class by making them private. Another thing you can do is to make the properties **immutable**, that is, unchangeable. By using immutable properties, you don't even have to make them private.

Making properties immutable

There are two ways to mark a variable immutable in Dart: `final` and `const`. However, since the compiler won't know what the properties are until runtime, your only choice here is to use `final`.

In the `User` class in **user.dart**, add the `final` keyword before both property declarations. Your code should look like this:

```
final String _name;
final int _id;
```

Adding `final` means that `_name` and `_id` can only be given a value once, that is, when the constructor is called. After the object has been created, those properties will be immutable. You should keep the `String` and `int` type annotations, because removing them would cause the compiler to fall back to `dynamic`.

Making classes immutable

If the objects of a particular class can never change, because all fields of the class are `final`, you can add `const` to the constructor to ensure that all instances of the class will be constants at compile-time.

Since both the fields of your `User` class are now `final`, this class is a good candidate for a compile-time constant.

Replace both constructors with the following:

```
const User({int id = 0, String name = 'anonymous'})
    : assert(id >= 0),
      _id = id,
      _name = name;

const User.anonymous() : this();
```

Note the `const` keyword in front of both constructors. In the first constructor, there used to be an `assert` statement for `name.isNotEmpty`, but unfortunately, this is a runtime check and not allowed for a compile-time constant, so that had to be removed.

Now you can declare your `User` objects as compile-time constants like so:

```
const user = User(id: 42, name: 'Ray');
const anonymousUser = User.anonymous();
```

Benefits of using const

In addition to being immutable, another benefit of const variables is that they're **canonical instances**, which means that no matter how many instances you create, as long as the properties used to create them are the same, Dart will only see a single instance. You could instantiate User.anonymous() a thousand times across your app without incurring the performance hit of having a thousand different objects.

> **Note**: Flutter uses this pattern frequently with its const widget classes in the user interface of your app. Since Flutter knows that the const widgets are immutable, it doesn't have to waste time recalculating and drawing the layout when it finds these widgets.

Make it your goal to use const objects and constructors as much as possible. It's a performance win!

Factory constructors

All of the constructors that you've seen up until now have been generative constructors. Dart also provides another type of constructor called a **factory constructor**.

A factory constructor provides more flexibility in how you create your objects. A generative constructor can only create a new instance of the class itself. However, factory constructors can return *existing* instances of the class, or even subclasses of it. (You'll learn about subclasses in Chapter 9.) This is useful when you want to hide the implementation details of a class from the code that uses it.

The factory constructor is basically a special method that starts with the factory keyword and returns an object of the class type. For example, you could add the following factory constructor to your User class:

```
factory User.ray() {
  return User(id: 42, name: 'Ray');
}
```

The factory method uses the generative constructor to create and return a new instance of User. You could also accomplish the same thing with a named constructor, though.

A more common example you'll see is using a factory constructor to make a `fromJson` method:

```
factory User.fromJson(Map<String, Object> json) {
  final userId = json['id'] as int;
  final userName = json['name'] as String;
  return User(id: userId, name: userName);
}
```

You would create a `User` object from the constructor like so:

```
final map = {'id': 10, 'name': 'Manda'};
final manda = User.fromJson(map);
```

As mentioned earlier, you'll learn how the `Map` collection works in Chapter 8. The thing to pay attention to now is that the factory constructor body allows you to perform some work before returning the new object, without exposing the inner wiring of that instantiation process to whoever is using the class. For example, you could create a `User.fromJson` constructor with a named constructor like so:

```
User.fromJson(Map<String, Object> json)
    : id = json['id'] as int,
      name = json['name'] as String;
```

However, besides adding some simple asserts to the initializer list, there isn't much else you can do to with `id` and `name`. With a factory constructor, though, you could do all kinds of validation, error checking and even modification of the arguments before creating the object. This is actually highly desireable in the case here because if `'id'` or `'String'` didn't exist in the map, then your app would crash because you aren't handling `null`.

> **Note**: Using a factory constructor over a named constructor can also help to prevent breaking changes for subclasses of your class. That topic is a little beyond the scope of this chapter, but you can read https://stackoverflow.com/a/66117859 for a longer explanation.

You'll see a few more uses of the factory constructor in the section below on static members.

Constructor summary

Since there are so many ways that constructors can vary, here's a brief comparison.

Constructors can be:

- Forwarding or non-forwarding

- Named or unnamed

- Generative or factory

- Constant or not constant

Take the following example:

```
const User(this.id, this.name);
```

This is a non-forwarding, unnamed, generative, const constructor.

Mini-exercises

Given the following class:

```
class Password {
  String value = '';
}
```

1. Make value a final variable, but not private.

2. Add a const constructor as the only way to initialize a Password object.

Dart objects

Objects act as *references* to the instances of the class in memory. That means if you assign one object to another, the other object simply holds a reference to the same object in memory — not a new instance.

So if you have a class like this:

```
class MyClass {
  var myProperty = 1;
}
```

And you instantiate it like so:

```
final myObject = MyClass();
final anotherObject = myObject;
```

Then `myObject` and `anotherObject` both reference the *same* place in memory. Changing `myProperty` in either object will affect the other, since they both reference the same instance:

```
print(myObject.myProperty);    // 1
anotherObject.myProperty = 2;
print(myObject.myProperty);    // 2
```

As you can see, changing the value of the property on `anotherObject` also changed it in `myObject`, as they are really just two names for the same object.

> **Note**: If you want to make an *actual* copy of the class — not just a copy of its reference in memory but a whole *new* object with a deep copy of all the data it contains — then you'll need to implement that mechanism yourself by creating a method in your class that builds up a whole new object.

If that still doesn't make sense, you can look forward to sitting down by the fire and listening to the story of *The House on Wenderlich Way* in Chapter 8, which will make this all clear, or at least help you see it from a different perspective.

For now, though, there are a few more improvements you can make to the `User` class.

Getters

Right now the `User` class fields are private:

```
class User {
  // ...
  final int _id;
  final String _name;
  // ...
}
```

That means there's no way to access the user ID and name outside of the class, which makes your object kind of useless. You can solve this problem by adding a **getter**, which is a special method that uses the `get` keyword before a property name and returns a value. This gives you, as the class author, some control over how people access and modify properties, instead of giving people raw and unfettered access.

In the `User` class, near the `_id` and `_name` properties, *add* the following lines:

```
int get id => _id;
String get name => _name;
```

The `get` keyword provides a public-facing property name; in this case, `id` and `name`. When you call the getter using its name, the `get` method returns a value. The two getter methods here are simply returning the `_id` and `_name` field values.

Now that the properties are exposed, you can use them like so:

```
const ray = User(id: 42, name: 'Ray');
print(ray.id);   // 42
print(ray.name); // Ray
```

Calculated properties

You can even create getters that aren't backed by a dedicated field value, but instead are calculated when called. Here's an example:

```
bool get isBigId => _id > 1000;
```

There's no internal variable named `isBigId` or `_isBigId`. Rather, the return value of `isBigId` is calculated when necessary.

All of the getters above use arrow syntax, but you could also use brace syntax with a `return` statement if you wanted to use more than a single line of code to calculate the return value.

Setters

If you need mutable data in a class, there's a special `set` method to go along with `get`.

Rather than modifying any of the existing fields of `User` to have a setter, here's a simple new class called `Email`:

```
class Email {
  var _address = '';

  String get value => _address;
  set value(String address) => _address = address;
}
```

The last line in the body is the setter, which starts with the `set` keyword. The name `value` is the same name that's used by the getter above it. The `set` method takes a parameter, which you can use to set some value. In this case, you're setting the email address.

You can now assign and retrieve the value of `_address` like this:

```
final email = Email();
email.value = 'ray@example.com';
final emailString = email.value;
```

The second line sets the internal `_address` field, and the third line gets it.

You can see how this could give you some extra control over what's assigned to your properties; for instance, you could sanitize input, check for properly formatted email addresses, and more.

Refactoring

You don't always need to use getters and setters explicitly. In fact, if all you're doing is shadowing some internal field variable, then you're better off just using a public variable.

Refactoring the Email class

Refactoring the `Email` class from above to use a public variable would look like this:

```
class Email {
  var value = '';
}
```

Dart implicitly generates the needed getters and setters for you. That's quite a bit more readable and it still works exactly the same:

```
final email = Email();
email.value = 'ray@example.com';
final emailString = email.value;
```

That's the beauty of how Dart handles class properties. You can change the internal implementation, without the external world being any the wiser.

If you only want a getter but not a setter, then just make the property `final`, which will also require adding a constructor to initialize the property:

```
class Email {
```

```
    Email(this.value);
    final value;
}
```

Since you added a constructor, that does affect the outside world when instantiating the object, but it's nothing different than what you've seen previously:

```
final email = Email('ray@example.com');
final emailString = email.value;
```

Retrieving value is still the same as before.

Refactoring User

You can use these same principles to refactor the User class. Replace the entire class with the following code:

```
class User {
  const User({this.id = 0, this.name = 'anonymous'})
      : assert(id >= 0);

  const User.anonymous() : this();

  final String name;
  final int id;

  String toJson() {
    return '{"id":$id,"name":"$name"}';
  }

  @override
  String toString() {
    return 'User(id: $id, name: $name)';
  }
}
```

Here's what changed:

- Since the getters were only shadowing internal private fields, it was cleaner to remove the fields and just use a final property. If you ever need to use hidden fields again later, you can do so without affecting how the class is used from the outside.

- Since you removed the private fields, setting them in the initializer list is no longer necessary.

- Because the properties are now public variables, you can use this.id and this.name to initialize them in the short-form constructor style.

"Why all the runaround?" you ask. "I could have done all this in the beginning."

True, true. But then you wouldn't have learned so much! :]

Static members

There is just one more thing to cover for your well-rounded foundation in Dart classes. That's the `static` keyword.

If you put `static` in front of a member variable or method, that causes the variable or method to belong to the *class* rather than the *instance*:

```
class SomeClass {
  static int myProperty = 0;
  static void myMethod() {
    print('Hello, Dart!');
  }
}
```

And you access them like so:

```
final value = SomeClass.myProperty;
SomeClass.myMethod();
```

In this case, you didn't have to instantiate an object to access `myProperty` or to call `myMethod`. Instead, you were able to use the class name directly to get the value and call the method.

The following sections will cover a few common use cases for static members.

Static variables

Static variables are often used for constants and in the singleton pattern.

Note: Variables are given different names according to where they belong or where they're located. Since static variables belong to the class, they're called **class variables**. Non-static member variables are called **instance variables** because they only have a value after an object is instantiated. Variables within a method are called **local variables**, and top-level variables outside of a class are called **global variables**.

Constants

You can define class constants by combining `static` and `const`. For example:

```
static const myConstant = '42';
```

Doing so in the `User` class would improve readability for the default user ID and name. Add the following two lines to the class body below the properties:

```
static const _anonymousId = 0;
static const _anonymousName = 'anonymous';
```

Replace the unnamed constructor with the following:

```
const User({
  this.id = _anonymousId,
  this.name = _anonymousName,
}) : assert(id >= 0);
```

While anonymous was already pretty readable, `_anonymousId` is much more meaningful than 0.

Singleton pattern

A second use of static variables is to create a **singleton** class. Singletons are a common design pattern where there is only ever one instance of an object. While some people debate their benefits, they do make certain tasks more convenient.

It's easy to create a singleton in Dart. You wouldn't want `User` to be a singleton, since you'll likely have lots of distinct users, requiring lots of distinct instances of `User`. However, you might want to create a singleton class as a database helper so that you can ensure that you don't open multiple connections to the database.

Here is what a basic singleton class would look like:

```
class MySingleton {
  MySingleton._();
  static final MySingleton instance = MySingleton._();
}
```

The `MySingleton._()` part is a private named constructor. Some people like to call it `_internal` to emphasize that it can't be called from the outside. The underscore makes it impossible to instantiate the class normally. However, the static property, which is only initialized once, provides a reference to the instantiated object.

> **Note**: Static fields and top-level variables, that is, global variables outside of a class, are **lazily initialized**. That means Dart doesn't actually calculate and assign their values until you use them the first time.

You would access the singleton like so:

```
final mySingleton = MySingleton.instance;
```

Since factory constructors don't need to return new instances of an object, you can also implement the singleton pattern with a factory constructor:

```
class MySingleton {
  MySingleton._();
  static final MySingleton _instance = MySingleton._();
  factory MySingleton() => _instance;
}
```

The advantage here is that you can hide the fact that it's a singleton from whoever uses it:

```
final mySingleton = MySingleton();
```

From the outside, this looks exactly like a normal object. This gives you the freedom to change it back into a generative constructor later without affecting the code in other parts of your project.

The last two sections have been about static variables. Next, you'll take a look at static methods.

Static methods

There are a few interesting things you can do with static methods.

Utility methods

One use for a static method is to create a utility or helper method that's associated with the class, but not associated with any particular instance.

In other languages, some developers like to group related static utility methods in classes to keep them organized. However, in Dart it's usually better to just put these utility methods in their own file as top-level functions. You can then import that file as a library wherever you need the utility methods contained within.

Creating new objects

You can also use static methods to create new instances of a class based on some input passed in. For example, you could use a static method to achieve precisely the same result as you did earlier with the `fromJson` factory constructor. Here's the static method version:

```
static User fromJson(Map<String, Object> json) {
  final userId = json['id'] as int;
  final userName = json['name'] as String;
  return User(id: userId, name: userName);
}
```

From the outside as well, you use it as you did with the factory version:

```
final map = {'id': 10, 'name': 'Manda'};
final manda = User.fromJson(map);
```

All this goes to show that there are often multiple ways of accomplishing the same thing.

Comparing static methods with factory constructors

Factory constructors in many ways are just like static methods, but there are a few differences:

- A factory constructor can only return an instance of the class type or subtype, while a static method can return anything. For example, a static method can be asynchronous and return a `Future`, which you'll learn about in Chapter 10, but a factory constructor can't do this.

- A factory constructor can be unnamed so that, from the caller's perspective, it looks exactly like calling a generative constructor. The singleton example above is an example of this. A static method, on the other hand, must have a name.

- A factory constructor can be `const` if it's a forwarding constructor, but a static method can't.

Challenges

Before moving on, here are some challenges to test your knowledge of classes and the components that make them up. It's best if you try to solve them yourself, but solutions are available if you get stuck. These are located with the supplementary materials for this book.

Challenge 1: Bert and Ernie

Create a Student class with final firstName and lastName String properties and a variable grade as an int property. Add a constructor to the class that initializes all the properties. Add a method to the class that nicely formats a Student for printing. Use the class to create students bert and ernie with grades of 95 and 85, respectively.

Challenge 2: Spheres

Create a Sphere class with a const constructor that takes a positive length radius as a named parameter. Add getters for the the volume and surface area but none for the radius. Don't use the dart:math package but store your own version of pi as a static constant. Use your class to find the volume and surface area of a sphere with a radius of 12.

Key points

- Classes package data and functions inside a single structure.

- Variables in a class are called fields, and public fields or getter methods are called properties.

- Functions in a class are called methods.

- You can customize how an object is printed by overriding the `toString` method.

- You create an object from a class by calling a constructor method.

- Generative constructors can be unnamed or named.

- Unnamed generative constructors have the same name as the class, while named generative constructors have an additional identifier after the class name.

- You can forward from one constructor to another by using the keyword `this`.

- Initializer lists allow you to check constructor parameters with `assert` and initialize field variables.

- Adding `const` to a constructor allows you to create immutable, canonical instances of the class.

- Factory constructors allow you to hide the implementation details of how you provide the class instance.

- Classes have getters and setters which you can customize without affecting how the object is used.

- Adding the `static` keyword to a property or method makes it belong to the class rather than the instance.

Where to go from here?

This chapter touched briefly on JSON as a standard way to serialize objects. You'll certainly be using JSON in the future, so you can visit json.org to learn more about this format and why it's gained so much traction as a standard.

This chapter also alluded briefly to concepts such as singletons and factories. These concepts are known collectively as **design patterns**. Although you don't need to know design patterns to code in Dart, understanding them will make you a better programmer. The most famous book on this topic is *Design Patterns* by "The Gang of Four", but there are many other excellent works. A simple search for **software design patterns** online will provide you with a wealth of information.

Chapter 7: Nullability

By Jonathan Sande

You know that game where you try to find the item that doesn't belong in a list? Here's one for you:

```
horse, camel, pig, cow, sheep, goat
```

Which one doesn't belong?

It's the third one, of course! The other animals are raised by nomadic peoples, but a pig is a farmer's animal — it doesn't do so well trekking across the steppe. About now you're probably muttering to yourself why your answer was just as good — like, a sheep is the only animal with wool, or something similar. If you got an answer that works, good job. Here's another one:

```
196, 144, 169, 182, 121
```

Did you get it? The answer is one hundred and eighty-two. All the other numbers are squares of integers.

One more:

```
3, null, 1, 7, 4, 5
```

And the answer is . . . null! All of the other items in the list are integers, but null isn't an integer.

What? Was that too easy?

Null overview

As out of place as null looks in that list of integers, many computer languages actually include it. In the past Dart did, too, but as of version 2.12, Dart decided to take null out of the list and only put it back if you allow Dart to do so. This feature is called **sound null safety**, but to find out what was so dangerous about null in the first place, you'll have to keep reading.

What null means

Null means "no value" or "absence of a value". It's quite useful to have such a concept. Imagine not having null at all. Say you ask a user for their postal code so that you can save it as an integer in your program:

```
int postalCode = 12345;
```

Everything will go fine until you get a user who doesn't have a postal code. Your program requires some value, though, so what do you give it? Maybe 0 or –1?

```
int postalCode = -1;
```

Choosing a number like –1, though, is somewhat arbitrary. You have to define it yourself to mean "no value" and then tell other people that's what it means.

```
// Hey everybody, -1 means that the user
// doesn't have a postal code. Don't forget!
int postalCode = -1;
```

On the other hand, if you can have a dedicated value called null, which everyone already understands to mean "no value", then you don't need to add comments explaining what it means.

```
int postalCode = null;
```

It's obvious here that there's no postal code. In versions of Dart prior to 2.12 that line of code worked just fine. However, now it's no longer allowed. You get the following error:

```
A value of type 'Null' can't be assigned to a variable of type
'int'.
```

What's wrong? Null is a useful concept to have! Why not allow it, Dart?

The problem with null

As useful as null is for indicating the absence of a value, developers do have a problem with it. The problem is that they tend to forget that it exists. And when developers forget about null, they don't handle it in their code. Those nulls are like little ticking time bombs ready to explode the code.

To see that in action, how about taking a trip back in time. Open **pubspec.yaml** and set the minimum Dart SDK version to 2.10:

```
environment:
  sdk: '>=2.10.0 <3.0.0'
```

Save the file and run dart pub get if needed.

Dart 2.10 was the version before sound null safety was introduced in Dart. This will allow you to see first hand what a rogue null can do.

Now open **starter.dart** or whatever file you have your main function in, and replace the contents of the file with the following code:

```
void main() {
  print(isPositive(3));  // true
  print(isPositive(-1)); // false
}

bool isPositive(int anInteger) {
  return !anInteger.isNegative;
}
```

Run that code and you'll get a result of true and false as expected. The isPositive method works fine as long as you give it integers. But what if you give it null?

Add the following line to the bottom of the main function:

```
print(isPositive(null));
```

Run that and your program will crash with the following error:

```
NoSuchMethodError: The getter 'isNegative' was called on null.
```

You learned above that null means "no value", which is true, semantically. However, the Dart keyword null actually is a value in the sense that it's an object. That is, the object null is the sole instance of the Null class. Because the Null class doesn't have a method called isNegative, you get a NoSuchMethodError when you try to call null.isNegative.

Now go back to **pubspec.yaml** and change the minimum Dart SDK version to 2.12, the first version that supported sound null safety:

```
environment:
  sdk: '>=2.12.0 <3.0.0'
```

Save the file and again run `dart pub get` if needed.

Now all of a sudden you have an error where you tried to call your function with `null`:

```
                 The argument type 'Null' can't be assigned to the parameter
                 type 'int'. dart(argument_type_not_assignable)
                 View Problem (⌥F8)   No quick fixes available
print(isPositive(null));
```

With the advent of Dart's sound null safety, you *can't* assign a `null` value to an `int` even if you wanted to. Eliminating the possibility of being surprised by `null` prevents a whole host of errors.

Delete that line with the null error. Problem solved.

But wait? Isn't null useful? What about a missing postal code?

Yes, null is useful and Dart has a solution.

> **Note**: As you saw above, Dart only applies sound null safety checks to your project if you set the minimum version to 2.12. While this isn't required, the benefits for preventing null errors make it highly recommended.

Nullable vs. non-nullable types

Starting with version 2.12, Dart separated its types into nullable and non-nullable. Nullable types end with a question mark (?) while non-nullable types do not.

Non-nullable types

Dart types are **non-nullable by default**. That means they're *guaranteed* to never contain the value `null`, which is the essence of the meaning of **sound** in the phrase "sound null safety". These types are easy to recognize because, unlike nullable types, they don't have a question mark at the end.

Here are some example values that non-nullable types could contain:

- **int**: 3, 1, 7, 4, 5

- **double**: 3.14159265, 0.001, 100.5

- **bool**: true, false

- **String**: 'a', 'hello', 'Would you like fries with that?'

- **User**: ray, vicki, anonymous

These are all acceptable ways to set the values:

```
int myInt = 1;
double myDouble = 3.14159265;
bool myBool = true;
String myString = 'Hello, Dart!';
User myUser = User(id: 42, name: 'Ray');
```

As you saw earlier, trying to set a non-nullable type to `null` is a compile-time error:

```
int postalCode = null; // error
```

Since only types that end in a question mark can potentially have a `null` value, every time you see a type without a question mark, you can be absolutely positive that it won't ever be `null`.

> **Note:** Well, a type without a question mark *could* be null if you use the `late` keyword, but technically this is opting out of sound null safety. It's also completely under your control. You'll learn about the `late` keyword at the end of this chapter.

Nullable types

A **nullable type** can contain the `null` value in addition to its own data type. You can easily tell the type is nullable because it ends with a question mark (?), which is like saying, "Maybe you've got the data you want or maybe you've got `null`. That's the question." Here are some example values that nullable types could contain:

- **int?**: 3, null, 1, 7, 4, 5

- **double?**: 3.14159265, 0.001, 100.5, null

- **bool?**: true, false, null

- **String?**: `'a'`, `'hello'`, `'Would you like fries with that?'`, `null`

- **User?**: `ray`, `vicki`, `anonymous`, `null`

That means you can set any of them to `null`:

```
int? myInt = null;
double? myDouble = null;
bool? myBool = null;
String? myString = null;
User? myUser = null;
```

The question mark at the end of `String?` isn't an operator acting on the `String` type. Rather, `String?` is a whole new type separate from `String`. `String?` means that the variable can either contain a `String` or it can be `null`.

Every non-nullable type in Dart has a corresponding nullable type: `int` and `int?`, `bool` and `bool?`, `User` and `User?`, `Object` and `Object?`. By choosing the type, you get to choose when you want to allow null values and when you don't.

> **Note**: The non-nullable type is a subtype of its nullable form. For example, `String` is a subtype of `String?` since `String?` can be a `String`.

For any nullable variable in Dart, if you don't initialize it with a value, it'll be given the default value of `null`.

Create three variables of different nullable types:

```
int? age;
double? height;
String? message;
```

Then print them:

```
print(age);
print(height);
print(message);
```

You'll see `null` for each value.

Mini-exercises

1. Create a `String?` variable called `profession`, but don't give it a value. Then you'll have `profession` null. :]

2. Give `profession` a value of "basketball player".

3. Write the following line and then hover your cursor over the variable name. What type does Dart infer `iLove` to be?

```
const iLove = 'Dart';
```

Handling nullable types

The big problem with the old nullable types in the past was how easy it was to forget to add code to handle `null` values. That's no longer true. Dart now makes it impossible to forget because you really can't do much at all with a nullable value until you've dealt with the possibility of `null`.

Try out this example:

```
String? name;
print(name.length);
```

Dart doesn't let you run that code, so there isn't even an opportunity to get a runtime `NoSuchMethodError` like before. Instead, Dart gives you a compile-time error:

```
The property 'length' can't be unconditionally accessed because
the receiver can be 'null'.
```

Compile-time errors are your friends because they're easy to fix. In the next few sections you'll see how to use the many tools Dart has to deal with null values.

Type promotion

The **Dart analyzer**, which is the tool that tells you what the compile-time errors and warning are, is smart enough to tell in a wide range of situations if a nullable variable is guaranteed to contain a non-null value or not.

Take the last example, but this time assign `name` a string literal on the line after declaring it:

```
String? name;
name = 'Ray';
print(name.length);
```

Even though the type is still nullable, Dart can see that name can't possibly be null because you assigned it a non-null value right before you used it. There's no need for you to explicitly "unwrap" name to get at its String value. Dart does this for you automatically. This is known as **type promotion**. Dart promotes the nullable and largely unusable String? type to a non-nullable String with no extra work from you! Your code stays clean and beautiful. Take some time right now to send the Dart team a thank you letter.

Flow analysis

Type promotion works for more than just the trivial example above. Dart uses sophisticated **flow analysis** to check every possible route the code could take. As long as none of the routes come up with the possibility of null, it's promotion time!

Take the following slightly less trivial example:

```
bool isPositive(int? anInteger) {
  if (anInteger == null) {
    return false;
  }
  return !anInteger.isNegative;
}
```

In this case, you can see that by the time you get to the anInteger.isNegative line, anInteger can't possibly be null because you've already checked for that. Dart's flow analysis could also see that, so Dart promoted anInteger to its non-nullable form, that is, to int instead of int?.

Even if you had a much longer and nested if-else chain, Dart's flow analysis would still be able to determine whether to promote a nullable type or not.

Null-aware operators

In addition to flow analysis, Dart also gives you a whole set of tools called **null-aware operators** that can help you handle potentially null values. Here they are in brief:

- If-null operator (??)

- Null-aware assignment operator (??=)

- Null-aware access operator (?.)

- Null-aware method invocation operator (?.)

- Null assertion operator (!)

- Null-aware cascade operator (?..)

- Null-aware index operator (?[])

- Null-aware spread operator (...?)

The following sections describe in more detail how these operators work.

If-null operator (??)

One very convenient way to handle null values is to use the double question mark (??), also known as the **if-null operator**. This operator says, "If the value on the left isn't null, then use it; otherwise, go with the value on the right."

Take a look at the following example:

```
String? message;
final text = message ?? 'Error';
```

Here are a couple points to note:

- Since message is null, ?? will set text equal to the right-hand value: 'Error'.

- Using ?? ensures that text can never be null, thus Dart infers the variable type of text to be String and not String?.

Print text to confirm that Dart assigned it the 'Error' string rather than null.

Using the ?? operator in this example is equivalent to the following:

```
String text;
if (message == null) {
  text = 'Error';
} else {
  text = message;
}
```

That's six lines of code instead of one when you use the ?? operator. You know which one to choose.

Null-aware assignment operator (??=)

In the example above, you had two variables: message and text. However, another common situation is when you have a single variable that you want to update if its value is null.

For example, say you have an optional font size setting in your app:

```
double? fontSize;
```

When it's time to apply the font size to the text, your first choice is to go with the user selected size. If they haven't chosen one, then you'll fall back on a default size of 20.0. One way to achieve that is by using the if-null operator like so:

```
fontSize = fontSize ?? 20.0;
```

However, there's an even more compact way to do it. In the same way that the following two forms are equivalent,

```
x = x + 1;
x += 1;
```

there's also a **null-aware assignment operator** (??=) to simplify if-null statements that have a single variable:

```
fontSize ??= 20.0;
```

If fontSize is null then it will be assigned 20.0, but otherwise it retains its value. The ??= operator combines the null check with the assignment.

Both ?? and ??= are useful for initializing variables when you want to guarantee a non-null value.

Null-aware access operator (?.)

Earlier with anInteger.isNegative, you saw that trying to access the isNegative property when anInteger was null caused a NoSuchMethodError. There's also an operator for null safety when accessing object members. The **null-aware access operator** returns null if the left-hand side is null. Otherwise, it returns the property on the right-hand side.

Look at the following example:

```
int? age;
print(age?.isNegative);
```

Since age is null, the ?. operator prevents that code from crashing. Instead, it just returns null for the whole expression inside the print statement. Run that and you'll see the following:

```
null
```

Internally, a property is just a getter method on an object, so the `?.` operator works the same way to call methods as it does to access properties.

Therefore, another name for `?.` is the **null-aware method invocation operator**. As you can see, invoking the `toDouble()` method works the same way as accessing the `isNegative` property:

```
print(age?.toDouble());
```

Run that and it'll again print "null" without an error.

The `?.` operator is useful if you want to only perform an action when the value is non-null. This allows you to gracefully proceed without crashing the app.

Null assertion operator (!)

Sometimes Dart isn't sure whether a nullable variable is `null` or not, but *you* know it's not. Dart is smart and all, but machines don't rule the world yet.

So if you're absolutely sure that a variable isn't `null`, you can turn it into a non-nullable type by using the **null assertion operator** (`!`), or sometimes more generally referred to as the **bang operator**.

```
String nonNullableString = myNullableString!;
```

Note the `!` at the end of `myNullableString`.

> **Note**: In Chapter 4, you learned about the not-operator, which is also an exclamation mark. To differentiate the not-operator from the null assertion operator, you can also refer to the not-operator as the **prefix ! operator** because it goes before an expression. By the same reasoning, you can refer to the null assertion operator as the **postfix ! operator** since it goes after an expression.

Here's an example to see the assertion operator at work. In your project, add the following function that returns a nullable Boolean:

```
bool? isBeautiful(String? item) {
  if (item == 'flower') {
    return true;
  } else if (item == 'garbage') {
    return false;
  }
```

```
    return null;
  }
```

Now in `main`, write this line:

```
bool flowerIsBeautiful = isBeautiful('flower');
```

You'll see this error:

```
A value of type 'bool?' can't be assigned to a variable of type
bool
```

The `isBeautiful` function returned a nullable type of `bool?`, but you're trying to assign it to `flowerIsBeautiful`, which has a non-nullable type of `bool`. The types are different, so you can't do that. However, you *know* that `'flower'` is beautiful, that is, the function won't return `null`. So you can use the null assertion operator to tell Dart that.

Add the postfix `!` operator to the end of the function call:

```
bool flowerIsBeautiful = isBeautiful('flower')!;
```

Now there are no more errors.

Alternatively, since `bool` is a subtype of `bool?`, you could also cast `bool?` down using the `as` keyword that you learned about in Chapter 3.

```
bool flowerIsBeautiful = isBeautiful('flower') as bool;
```

This is equivalent to using the assertion operator. The advantage of `!` is that it's shorter.

Beware, though. Using the assertion operator (or casting down to a non-nullable type) will crash your app with a runtime error if the value actually does turn out to be `null`, so don't use the assertion operator unless you can guarantee that the variable isn't `null`.

It's not really safe to trust the `isBeautiful` function. Who knows but that one day you'll hire someone who hates flowers and changes the internal workings of the function. That scenario isn't as far-fetched as you might think. Imagine that instead of working with a local function, you're returning data from a web server using a REST API. Someone on the server end changes a value and then your app breaks.

Here's an alternative to the assertion operator that won't ever crash the app:

```
bool flowerIsBeautiful = isBeautiful('flower') ?? true;
```

You're leaving the decision up to the function, but giving it a default value by using the ?? operator if the function doesn't know what it should be.

Think of the ! assertion operator as a dangerous option and one to be used sparingly. By using the assertion operator, you're telling Dart that you want to opt-out of null safety, that you can handle it yourself. This is something akin to using dynamic to tell Dart that you want to opt-out of type safety.

> **Note**: You'll see a common and valid use of the null assertion operator in the section below titled **No promotion for non-local variables**.

Null-aware cascade operator (?..)

In Chapter 6 you learned about the **cascade operator** (..), which allows you to call multiple methods or set multiple properties on the same object.

Give a class like this:

```
class User {
  String? name;
  int? id;
}
```

If you know the object isn't nullable, you can use the cascade operator like so:

```
User user = User()
  ..name = 'Ray'
  ..id = 42;
```

However, if your object *is* nullable, like in the following example:

```
User? user;
```

Then you can use the **null-aware cascade operator** (?..):

```
user
  ?..name = 'Ray'
  ..id = 42;
```

You only need to use ?.. for the first item in the chain. If user is null, then the chain will be **short-circuited**, that is, terminated, without calling the other items in the cascade chain.

This is similar for the null-aware access operator (?.) as well. Look at this example:

```
String? lengthString = user?.name?.length.toString();
```

Since user might be null, it needs the ?. operator to access name. Since name also might be null, it needs the ?. operator to access length. However, as long as name isn't null, length will never be null, so you only use the . dot operator to call toString. If either user or name is null, then the entire chain is immediately short-circuited and lengthString is assigned null.

Null-aware index operator (?[])

The **null-aware index operator** (?[]) is used for accessing the elements of a list when the list itself might be null. You've used lists already a couple of times in this book, but since you won't cover them in depth until Chapter 8, this section will just give a simple explanation of how the ?[] operator is used.

This is an example of a nullable list:

```
List<int>? myList = [1, 2, 3];
```

What you have here is a list of integers. The list itself can be set to null, indicated by the question mark at the end of List<int>?. However, the members of the list can't be null, indicated by the lack of a question mark after int. That is, the type is List<int>? instead of List<int?>?.

In the example above, myList isn't null because you assigned it the value [1, 2, 3]. Now set myList to null:

```
myList = null;
```

Try to get the value of one of the items in the list:

```
int? myItem = myList?[2];
```

Print myItem and you'll see null.

If you had tried to retrieve a value from a null list in the days before null safety, you would have crashed your app. However, the ?[] operator gracefully passes a null value on to myItem.

In Chapter 8 you'll learn more about collections, including the **null-aware spread operator** (...?), which is used to expand one non-null collection inside another.

Initializing non-nullable fields

When you create an object from a class, Dart requires you to initialize any non-nullable member variables before you use them.

Say you have a User class like this:

```
class User {
  String name;
}
```

Since name is String and not String?, you must initialize it somehow. If you recall what you learned in Chapter 6, there are a few different ways to do that.

Using initializers

One way to initialize a property is to use an **initializer** value:

```
class User {
  String name = 'anonymous';
}
```

In this example, the value is 'anonymous', so Dart knows that name will always get a non-null value when an object is created from this class.

Using initializing formals

Another way to initialize a property is to use an **initializing formal**, that is, by using this in front of the field name:

```
class User {
  User(this.name);
  String name;
}
```

Having this.name as a required parameter ensures that name will have a non-null value.

Using an initializer list

You can also use an **initializer list** to set a field variable:

```
class User {
  User(String name)
    : _name = name;
  String _name;
}
```

The private _name field is guaranteed to get a value when the constructor is called.

Using default parameter values

Optional parameters default to null if you don't set them, so for non-nullable types, that means you *must* provide a default value.

You can set a default value for ordered parameters like so:

```
class User {
  User([this.name = 'anonymous']);
  String name;
}
```

Or like this for named parameters:

```
class User {
  User({this.name = 'anonymous'});
  String name;
}
```

Now even when creating an object without any parameters, name will still at least have a default value.

Required named parameters

As you learned in Chapter 5, if you want to make a named parameter required, use the required keyword.

```
class User {
  User({required this.name});
  String name;
}
```

Since name is required, there's no need to provide a default value.

Nullable instance variables

All of the methods above guaranteed that the class field will be initialized, and not only initialized, but initialized with a non-null value. Since the field is non-nullable, it's not even possible to make the following mistake:

```
final user = User(name: null);
```

Dart won't let you do that. You'll get the following compile-time error:

```
The argument type 'Null' can't be assigned to the parameter type
'String'
```

Of course, if you want the property to be nullable, then you can use a nullable type, and then there's no need to initialize the value.

```
class User {
  User({this.name});
  String? name;
}
```

`String?` makes name nullable. Now it's your responsibility to handle any `null` values it may contain.

No promotion for non-local variables

One topic that people often get confused about is the lack of type promotion for nullable instance variables.

As you recall from earlier, Dart promotes nullable variables in a method to their non-nullable counterpart if Dart's flow analysis can guarantee the variable will never be null:

```
bool isLong(String? text) {
  if (text == null) {
    return false;
  }
  return text.length > 100;
}
```

In this example, the local variable `text` is guaranteed to be non-null if the line with `text.length` is ever reached, so Dart promotes `text` from `String?` to `String`.

However, take a look at this modified example:

```
class TextWidget {
  String? text;

  bool isLong() {
    if (text == null) {
      return false;
    }
    return text.length > 100; // error
  }
}
```

The line with `text.length` now gives an error:

```
The property 'length' can't be unconditionally accessed because
the receiver can be 'null'.
```

Why is that? You just checked for `null` after all.

The reason is that the Dart compiler can't guarantee that other methods or subclasses won't change the value of a non-local variable before it's used.

Since Dart has gone the path of *sound* null safety, this guarantee is essential before type promotion can happen.

You do have options, however. One is to use the `!` operator:

```
bool isLong() {
  if (text == null) {
    return false;
  }
  return text!.length > 100;
}
```

Even if the compiler don't know that text isn't null, *you* know it's not, so you apply that knowledge with `text!`.

Another option is to shadow the non-local variable with a local one:

```
class TextWidget {
  String? text;

  bool isLong() {
    final text = this.text; // shadowing
    if (text == null) {
      return false;
    }
    return text.length > 100;
```

```
    }
  }
```

The local variable `text` shadows the instance variable `this.text` and the compiler is happy.

> **Note**: The topic of type promotion for non-local variables is in active discussion at the time of writing this chapter. It may be that when you read this Dart will have an updated solution.

The late keyword

Sometimes you want to use a non-nullable type, but you can't initialize it in any of the ways you learned above.

Here's an example:

```dart
class User {
  User(this.name);

  final String name;
  final int _secretNumber = _calculateSecret();

  int _calculateSecret() {
    return name.length + 42;
  }
}
```

You have this non-nullable field named `_secretNumber`. You want to initialize it based on the return value from a complex algorithm in the `_calculateSecret` instance method. You have a problem, though, because Dart doesn't let you access instance methods during initialization.

```
The instance member '_calculateSecret' can't be accessed in an
initializer.
```

To solve this problem, you can use the `late` keyword. Add `late` to the start of the line initializing `_secretNumber`:

```dart
late final int _secretNumber = _calculateSecret();
```

Dart accepts it now, and there are no more errors.

Using `late` means that Dart doesn't initialize the variable right away. It only initializes it when you access it the first time. This is also known as **lazy initialization**. It's like procrastination for variables.

It's also common to use `late` to initialize a field variable in the constructor body. Here's an alternate version of the example above:

```
class User {
  User(this.name) {
    _secretNumber = _calculateSecret();
  }
  late final int _secretNumber;
  // ...
}
```

Initializing a final variable in the constructor body wouldn't have been allowed if it weren't marked as `late`.

Dangers of being late

The example above was for initializing a final variable, but you can also use `late` with non-final variables. You have to be careful with this, though. Take a look at the following example:

```
class User {
  late String name;
}
```

Dart doesn't complain at you, because using `late` means that you're promising Dart that you'll initialize the field before it's ever used. This moves checking from compile-time to runtime.

Now add the following code to `main` and run it:

```
final user = User();
print(user.name);
```

You broke your word and never initialized `name` before you used it. Dart is disappointed with you, and complains accordingly:

```
LateInitializationError: Field 'name' has not been initialized.
```

For this reason, it's somewhat dangerous to use `late` when you're not initializing it either in the constructor body or in the same line that you declare it.

Like with the null assertion operator (!), using `late` sacrifices the assurances of sound null safety and puts the responsibility of handling `null` into your hands. If you mess up, that's on you.

Benefits of being lazy

Who knew that it pays to be lazy sometimes? Dart knows this, though, and uses it to great advantage.

There are times when it might take some heavy calculations to initialize a variable. If you never end up using the variable, then all that initialization work was a waste. Since *lazy* initialization is never done until you actually use the variable, though, this kind of work will never be wasted.

Top-level and static variables have always been lazy in Dart. As you learned above, the `late` keyword makes other variables lazy, too. That means even if your variable is nullable, you can still use `late` to get the benefit of making it lazy.

Here's what that would look like:

```
class SomeClass {
  late String? value = doHeavyCalculation();
  String? doHeavyCalculation() {
    // do heavy calculation
  }
}
```

The method `doHeavyCalculation` is only run after you access `value` the first time. And if you never access it, you never do the work.

Well, that wraps up this chapter. Sound null safety has made Dart an even stronger language than it already was. Aren't you glad you chose to learn Dart?

Challenges

Before moving on, here are some challenges to test your knowledge of nullability. It's best if you try to solve them yourself, but solutions are available with the supplementary materials for this book if you get stuck.

Challenge 1: Random nothings

Write a function that randomly returns 42 or null. Assign the return value of the function to a variable named result that will never be null. Give result a default of 0 if the function returns null.

Challenge 2: Naming customs

People around the world have different customs for giving names to children. It would be difficult to create a data class to accurately represent them all, but try it like this:

- Create a class called Name with givenName and surname properties.

- Some people write their surname last and some write it first. Add a Boolean property called surnameIsFirst to keep track of this.

- Not everyone in the world has a surname.

- Add a toString method that prints the full name.

Key points

- Null means "no value."

- A common cause of errors for programming languages in general comes from not properly handling null.

- Dart 2.12 introduced sound null safety to the language.

- Sound null safety distinguishes nullable and non-nullable types.

- A non-nullable type is guaranteed to never be null.

- Null aware operators help developers to gracefully handle null.

```
??     if-null operator
??=    null-aware assignment operator
?.     null-aware access operator
?.     null-aware method invocation operator
!      null assertion operator
?..    null-aware cascade operator
?[]    null-aware index operator
...?   null-aware spread operator
```

- The late keyword allows you to delay initializing a field in a class.

- Using late also makes initialization lazy, so a variable's value won't be calculated until you access the variable for the first time.

Where to go from here?

Dart is an evolving and ever improving language. Since development and discussions about new features all happen out in the open, you can watch and even participate. Go to dart.dev/community to learn more.

Chapter 8: Collections

By Jonathan Sande

In almost every application you make, you'll be dealing with collections of data. Data can be organized in multiple ways, each with a different purpose. Dart provides multiple solutions to fit your collection's needs, and in this chapter you'll learn about three of the main ones: lists, sets and maps.

Lists

Whenever you have a very large collection of objects of a single type that have an ordering associated with them, you'll likely want to use a **list** as the data structure for ordering the objects. Lists in Dart are similar to arrays in other languages.

The image below represents a list with six **elements**. Lists are zero-based, so the first element is at **index 0**. The **value** of the first element is cake, the value of the second element is pie, and so on until the last element at index 5, which is cookie.

The order of a list matters. Pie is after cake, but before donut. If you loop through the list multiple times, you can be sure the elements will stay in the same location and order.

Basic list operations

You'll start by learning how to create lists and modify elements.

Creating a list

You can create a list by specifying the initial elements of the list within square brackets. This is called a **list literal**.

```
var desserts = ['cookies', 'cupcakes', 'donuts', 'pie'];
```

Since all of the elements in this list are strings, Dart infers this to be a list of `String` types.

You can reassign `desserts` (but why would one ever want to reassign desserts?) with an empty list like so:

```
desserts = [];
```

Dart still knows that `desserts` is a list of strings. However, if you were to initialize a new empty list like this:

```
var snacks = [];
```

Dart wouldn't have enough information to know what kind of objects the list should hold. In this case, Dart simply infers it to be a list of `dynamic`. This causes you to lose type safety, which you don't want. If you're starting with an empty list, you should specify the type like so:

```
List<String> snacks = [];
```

There are a couple of details to note here:

- `List` is the data type, or class name, as you learned in Chapter 6.

- The angle brackets < > here are the notation for **generic types** in Dart. A generic list means you can have a list of anything; you just put the type you want inside the angle brackets. In this case, you have a list of strings, but you could replace `String` with any other type. For example, `List<int>` would make a list of integers, `List<bool>` would make a list of Booleans, and `List<Grievance>` would make a list of grievances — but you'd have to define that type yourself since Dart doesn't come with any by default.

A slightly nicer syntax for creating an empty list is to use `var` or `final` and move the generic type to the right:

```
var snacks = <String>[];
```

Dart still has all the information it needs to know this is an empty list of type `String`.

Printing lists

As you can do with any collection, you can print the contents of a list by using the `print` statement. Since `desserts` is currently empty, give it a list with elements again so that you have something interesting to show when you print it out.

```
desserts = ['cookies', 'cupcakes', 'donuts', 'pie'];
print(desserts);
```

Run that and you'll see the following:

```
[cookies, cupcakes, donuts, pie]
```

Accessing elements

To access the elements of a list, you reference its index via **subscript notation**, where the index number goes within square brackets after the list name.

```
final secondElement = desserts[1];
print(secondElement);
```

Don't forget that lists are zero-based, so index 1 fetches the second element. Run that code and you'll see `cupcakes` as expected.

If you know the value but don't know the index, you can use the `indexOf` method to look it up:

```
final index = desserts.indexOf('pie');
final value = desserts[index];
```

Since `'pie'` is the fourth item in the zero-based list, `index` is 3 and `value` is `pie`.

Assigning values to list elements

Just as you access elements, you also assign values to specific elements using subscript notation:

```
desserts[1] = 'cake';
```

This changes the value at index 1 from `cupcakes` to `cake`.

Adding elements to a list

Lists are growable by default in Dart, so you can use the `add` method to add an element.

```
desserts.add('brownies');
print(desserts);
```

Run that and you'll see:

```
[cookies, cake, donuts, pie, brownies]
```

Now `desserts` has five elements and the last one is `brownies`.

Removing elements from a list

You can remove elements using the `remove` method. So if you'd gotten a little hungry and eaten the cake, you'd write:

```
desserts.remove('cake');
print(desserts);
```

This leaves a list with four elements:

```
[cookies, donuts, pie, brownies]
```

No worries, there's still plenty for a midnight snack tonight!

Mutable and immutable lists

In the examples above, you were able to reassign list literals to desserts like so:

```
var desserts = ['cookies', 'cupcakes', 'donuts', 'pie'];
desserts = [];
desserts = ['cookies', 'cupcakes', 'donuts', 'pie'];
```

The reason you could do that is because you defined `desserts` using the `var` keyword. This has nothing to do with the list itself being immutable or not. It only means that you can swap out *different* lists in `desserts`.

Now try the following using `final`:

```
final desserts = ['cookies', 'cupcakes', 'donuts', 'pie'];
desserts = [];                      // not allowed
desserts = ['cake', 'ice cream'];   // not allowed
desserts = someOtherList;           // not allowed
```

Unlike `var`, using `final` means that you're not allowed to use the assignment operator to give `desserts` a new list.

However, look at this:

```
final desserts = ['cookies', 'cupcakes', 'donuts', 'pie'];
desserts.remove('cookies');    // OK
desserts.remove('cupcakes');   // OK
desserts.add('ice cream');     // OK
```

Obviously, the `final` keyword isn't keeping you from changing the contents of the list elements. What's happening?

Perhaps a little story will help.

The House on Wenderlich Way

You live in a house at 321 Lonely Lane. All you have at home are a few brownies, which you absentmindedly munch on as you scour the internet in hopes of finding work. Finally, you get a job as a senior Flutter developer, so you buy a new house at 122 Wenderlich Way. Best of all, your neighbor Ray brings over some cookies, cupcakes, donuts and pie as a house warming gift! The brownies are still at your old place, but in your excitement about the move you've forgotten all about them.

Using `var` is like giving you permission to move houses. The first house had brownies. The second house had cookies, cupcakes, donuts and pie. Different houses, different desserts.

Using `final`, on the other hand, is like saying, "Here's your house, but this is the last place you can ever live." However, just because you live at a fixed location doesn't mean that you can't change what's inside the house. You might live permanently at 122 Wenderlich Way, but it's fine to eat all the cookies and cupcakes in the house and then go to the store and bring home some ice cream. Well, it's fine in that it's permissible, but maybe you should pace yourself a little on the sweets.

So too with a `final` list. Even though the memory address is constant, the values at that address are mutable. Mutable data is nice and all, but when you open your cupboard expecting to find donuts but instead discover the neighbor kids traded them for slugs, it's not so pleasant. It's the same with lists — sometimes you just don't want to be surprised.

So how do you get an immutable list? Have you already guessed the answer? Good job if you have!

Creating deeply immutable lists

The solution to creating an immutable list is to mark the variable name with the `const` keyword. This forces the list to be **deeply immutable**.

That is, every element of the list must also be a compile-time constant.

```
const desserts = ['cookies', 'cupcakes', 'donuts', 'pie'];
desserts.add('brownie'); // not allowed
desserts.remove('pie');  // not allowed
desserts[0] = 'fudge';   // not allowed
```

Since `const` precedes `desserts` in the example above, you're not allowed to add to, remove from, or update the list.

If you aren't able to use `const` for the variable itself, you can still make the value deeply immutable by adding the optional `const` keyword before the value.

```
final desserts = const ['cookies', 'cupcakes', 'donuts', 'pie'];
```

Finally, if you want an immutable list but you won't know the element values until runtime, then you can create one with the `List.unmodifiable` named constructor:

```
final modifiableList = [DateTime.now(), DateTime.now()];
final unmodifiableList = List.unmodifiable(modifiableList);
```

`DateTime.now()` returns the date and time when it's called. You're obviously not going to know that until runtime, so this prevents the list from taking `const`. Passing that list into `List.unmodifiable`, however, makes the new list immutable.

> **Note**: Unfortunately, inadvertently trying to modify an unmodifiable list will cause a runtime error — not a compile-time error. So while mutable data can be unsafe, so too can unmodifiable lists. A good practice is to write tests to ensure your code works as intended.

That's enough about mutability for now. Next you'll see some properties you can access on lists.

List properties

Collections such as List have a number of properties. To demonstrate them, use the following list of drinks.

```
const drinks = ['water', 'milk', 'juice', 'soda'];
```

Accessing first and last elements

You can access the first and last element in a list:

```
drinks.first   // water
drinks.last    // soda
```

Checking if a list contains any elements

You can also check whether a list is empty or not empty.

```
drinks.isEmpty     // false
drinks.isNotEmpty  // true
```

This is equivalent to the following:

```
drinks.length == 0 // false
drinks.length > 0  // true
```

However, it's more readable to use isEmpty and isNotEmpty.

Looping over the elements of a list

For this section you can return to your list of desserts:

```
const desserts = ['cookies', 'cupcakes', 'donuts', 'pie'];
```

In Chapter 4, you saw how to iterate over lists, so this is a review of the for-in loop.

```
for (var dessert in desserts) {
  print(dessert);
}
```

Each time through the loop, `dessert` is assigned an element from `desserts`.

You also saw how to use `forEach` with an anonymous function.

```
desserts.forEach((dessert) => print(dessert));
```

And since the input of `print` is the same as the output of the `forEach` function, Dart allows you to rephrase that like so:

```
desserts.forEach(print);
```

This is known as a **tear-off** because you *tear off* the unnecessary syntax.

Run any of the loops above and you'll get the same result.

```
cookies
cupcakes
donuts
pie
```

Code as UI

The Flutter framework chose Dart because of its unique characteristics. However, Flutter has also influenced the development of Dart. One area you can see this is with the addition of the **spread operator**, **collection `if`** and **collection `for`**.

They make it easier for Flutter developers to compose user interface layouts completely in code, without the need for a separate markup language.

Flutter UI code is composed of classes called **widgets**. Three common Flutter widgets are rows, columns and stacks, which all store their children as `List` collections. Being able to manipulate lists using the spread operator, collection `if` and collection `for` makes it easier to build the UI with code.

The examples below use strings, but in a Flutter app you would see the same things with lists of `Text`, `Icon`, `ElevatedButton` and other `Widget` elements.

Spread operator

Suppose you have two lists to start with.

```
const pastries = ['cookies', 'croissants'];
const candy = ['Junior Mints', 'Twizzlers', 'M&Ms'];
```

You can use the **spread operator** (`...`) to expand those lists into another list.

```
const desserts = ['donuts', ...pastries, ...candy];
print(desserts);
```

By using the `...` operator, the second element of `desserts` is not `pastries`, but instead, the elements of `pastries` are themselves the elements of `desserts`. The same goes for candy. Run that code and you'll see the following:

```
[donuts, cookies, croissants, Junior Mints, Twizzlers, M&Ms]
```

There's also a **null spread operator** (`...?`), which will omit a list if the list itself is `null`.

```
List<String>? coffees;
final hotDrinks = ['milk tea', ...?coffees];
```

Here `coffees` has not been initialized and therefore is `null`. By using the `...?` operator, you avoid an error that would come by trying to add a null list. The list `hotDrinks` will only include `milk tea`.

Collection if

When creating a list, you can use a **collection if** to determine whether an element is included based on some condition.

So if you had a peanut allergy, you'd want to avoid adding certain candy with peanut butter to a list of candy.

```
const peanutAllergy = true;

const candy = [
  'Junior Mints',
  'Twizzlers',
  if (!peanutAllergy) 'Reeses',
];
print(candy);
```

Run that and you'll see that the `false` condition for the collection `if` prevented Reeses from being included in the list:

```
[Junior Mints, Twizzlers]
```

It's also interesting to note that collection `if` doesn't prevent a list from being a compile-time constant, as demonstrated by the presence of the `const` keyword.

Collection for

There's also a **collection for**. So if you have a list, you can use a collection `for` to iterate over the list and generate another list.

```
const deserts = ['gobi', 'sahara', 'arctic'];
var bigDeserts = [
  'ARABIAN',
  for (var desert in deserts) desert.toUpperCase(),
];
print(bigDeserts);
```

Here you've created a new list where the final three elements are the uppercase version of the elements from the input list. The syntax is very much like a `for-in` loop but without the braces.

Run the code to see:

```
[ARABIAN, GOBI, SAHARA, ARCTIC]
```

Before moving on to learn about the `Set` collection type, test your knowledge so far with some mini-exercises.

Mini-exercises

1. Create an empty list of type `String`. Name it `months`. Use the `add` method to add the names of the twelve months.

2. Make an immutable list with the same elements as in Mini-exercise 1.

3. Use collection `for` to create a new list with the month names in all uppercase.

Sets

Sets are used to create a collection of unique elements. Sets in Dart are similar to their mathematical counterparts. Duplicates are not allowed in a set, in contrast to lists, which do allow duplicates.

You can also think of sets as a bag of elements with no particular ordering, unlike lists, which do maintain a specific order. Because order doesn't matter in a set, sets can be faster than lists, especially when dealing with large datasets.

Creating a set

You can create an empty set in Dart using the Set type annotation like so:

```
final Set<int> someSet = {};
```

The generic syntax with int in angle brackets tells Dart that only integers are allowed in the set. The following form is shorter but identical in result:

```
final someSet = <int>{};
```

The curly braces are the same symbols used for sets in mathematics, so that should help you remember them. Be sure to distinguish curly braces in this context from their use for defining scopes, though.

You can also use type inference with a **set literal** to let Dart determine the types of elements in the set.

```
final anotherSet = {1, 2, 3, 1};
print(anotherSet);
```

Since the set literal contains only integers, Dart is able to infer the type as Set<int>.

Additionally, you probably noticed that there are two 1s there. But because anotherSet is a set, it ends up with only one 1. Run that code to verify the contents of anotherSet has only one 1.

```
{1, 2, 3}
```

Operations on a set

In this section you'll see some general collection operations that also apply to sets.

Checking the contents

To see if a set contains an item, you use the contains method, which returns a bool.

Add the following two lines and run the code again:

```
print(anotherSet.contains(1));   // true
print(anotherSet.contains(99)); // false
```

Since `anotherSet` does contains 1, the method returns `true`, while checking for 99 returns `false`.

Adding single elements

Like growable lists, you can add and remove elements in a set. To add an element, use the add method.

```
final someSet = <int>{};
someSet.add(42);
someSet.add(2112);
someSet.add(42);
print(someSet);
```

Run that to see the following set:

```
{42, 2112}
```

You added 42 twice, but only one 42 shows up as expected.

Removing elements

You can also remove elements using the `remove` method.

```
someSet.remove(2112);
```

Print `someSet` to reveal only a single element is left:

```
{42}
```

Adding multiple elements

You can use `addAll` to add elements from a list into a set.

```
someSet.addAll([1, 2, 3, 4]);
```

Print `someSet` again to show the new contents:

```
{42, 1, 2, 3, 4}
```

Intersections and Unions

You'll often have multiple sets of data and you'll want to know how they fit together.

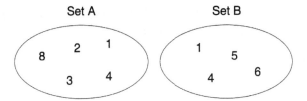

You've probably seen your share of Venn diagrams; if not in school, then at least as memes on the internet. They're useful for showing the common elements between two sets.

As you can see, 1 and 4 are in both sets.

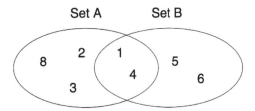

Intersections

Like Venn diagrams and mathematical sets, you can find the **intersection** of two sets in Dart; that is, the common elements that occur in both sets.

Given the following two sets:

```
final setA = {8, 2, 3, 1, 4};
final setB = {1, 6, 5, 4};
```

You can find the intersection like so:

```
final intersection = setA.intersection(setB);
```

Since both sets share the numbers 1 and 4, that's the answer you're expecting. Print `intersection` to see:

```
{1, 4}
```

No disappointments there.

Unions

Finding all the unique values by combining both sets gives you the **union**, and that's just as easy to find in Dart as the intersection.

```
final union = setA.union(setB);
```

Print `union` to see the results:

```
{8, 2, 3, 1, 4, 6, 5}
```

This union represents all the elements from both sets. Remember — sets have no requirement to be in order.

Other operations

Almost everything that you learned earlier about lists also applies to sets. Specifically, you can perform any of the following operations with sets:

- collection `if`
- collection `for`
- `for-in` loops
- `forEach` loops
- spread operators

Next you'll learn about another important collection type: maps.

Maps

Maps in Dart are the data structure used to hold key-value pairs. They're similar to HashMaps and Dictionaries in other languages.

If you're not familiar with maps, though, you can think of them like a collection of variables that contain data. The **key** is the variable name and the **value** is the data that the variable holds. The way to find a particular value is to give the map the name of the key that is *mapped* to that value.

In the image below, the cake is mapped to 500 calories, and the donut is mapped to 150 calories. cake and donut are keys, while 500 and 150 are values.

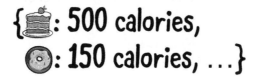

Map<Food, Calories>
Key type   Value type

The key and value in each pair are separated by colons, and consecutive key-value pairs are separated by commas.

Creating an empty map

Like List and Set, Map is a generic type, but Map takes two type parameters: one for the key and one for the value. You can create an empty map variable using Map and specifying the type for both the key and value:

```
final Map<String, int> emptyMap = {};
```

In this example, String is the type for the key, and int is the type for the value.

A slightly shorter way to do the same thing is move the generic types to the right-hand side:

```
final emptyMap = <String, int>{};
```

Notice that maps also use curly braces just as sets do. What do you think you'd get if you wrote this?

```
final emptySomething = {};
```

Is emptySomething a set, or is it a map?

Well, it turns out that map literals came before set literals in Dart's history, so Dart infers the empty braces to be a Map of <dynamic, dynamic>; that is, the types of the key and value are both dynamic. If you want a set, and not a map, then you need to be explicit:

```
final mySet = <String>{};
```

Like lists, maps have a length, which tells you the number of key-value pairs stored in the map.

```
final emptyMap = <String, int>{};
print(emptyMap.length);
```

Since it's an empty map, when you print that, you'll get 0 for the length.

Initializing a Map with values

You can create a non-empty map variable using braces, where Dart infers the key and value types. Dart knows it's a map because each element is a pair separated by a colon.

```
final inventory = {
  'cakes': 20,
  'pies': 14,
  'donuts': 37,
  'cookies': 141,
};
```

In this case, inventory is a map of String to int, from bakery item to quantity in stock.

The key doesn't have to be a string. For example, here's a map of int to String, from a digit to its English spelling:

```
final digitToWord = {
  1: 'one',
  2: 'two',
  3: 'three',
  4: 'four',
};
```

Print both of those:

```
print(inventory);
print(digitToWord);
```

You'll see the output in horizontal format rather than the vertical format you had above:

```
{cakes: 20, pies: 14, donuts: 37, cookies: 141}
{1: one, 2: two, 3: three, 4: four}
```

Unique keys

The keys of a map should be unique. A map like the following wouldn't work:

```
final treasureMap = {
  'garbage': 'in the dumpster',
  'glasses': 'on your head',
  'gold': 'in the cave',
  'gold': 'under your mattress',
};
```

There are two keys named gold. How are you going to know where to look? You're probably thinking, "Hey, it's gold. I'll just look both places." If you really wanted to set it up like that, then you could map String to List:

```
final treasureMap = {
  'garbage': ['in the dumpster'],
  'glasses': ['on your head'],
  'gold': ['in the cave', 'under your mattress'],
};
```

Now every key contains a list of items, but the keys themselves are unique.

Values don't have that same restriction of being unique. This is fine:

```
final myHouse = {
  'bedroom': 'messy',
  'kitchen': 'messy',
  'living room': 'messy',
  'code': 'clean',
};
```

Operations on a map

Interacting with a map to access, add, remove and update elements is very similar to what you've already seen.

Accessing elements from a map

You access individual elements from a map by using a subscript notation similar to lists, except for maps you use the key rather than an index.

```
final numberOfCakes = inventory['cakes'];
```

If you recall from above, the key `cakes` is mapped to the integer 20, so print `numberOfCakes` to see 20.

A map will return `null` if the key doesn't exist. Because of this, accessing an element from a map always gives a nullable value. In the example above, Dart infers `numberOfCakes` to be of type `int?`. If you want to use `numberOfCakes`, then you need to treat it as you would any other nullable value.

In this case you can use the null-aware access operator to check if the number of cakes is even:

```
print(numberOfCakes?.isEven);
```

There were 20 so that's `true`.

Adding elements to a map

You can add new elements to a map simply by assigning to elements that are not yet in the map.

```
inventory['brownies'] = 3;
```

Print `inventory` to see brownies and its value at the end of the map:

```
{cakes: 20, pies: 14, donuts: 37, cookies: 141, brownies: 3}
```

Updating an element

Remember that the keys of a map are unique, so if you assign a value to a key that already exists, you'll overwrite the existing value.

```
inventory['cakes'] = 1;
```

Print `inventory` to confirm that cakes was 20 but now is 1:

```
{cakes: 1, pies: 14, donuts: 37, cookies: 141, brownies: 3}
```

Removing elements from a map

You can use `remove` to remove elements from a map by key.

```
inventory.remove('cookies');
```

COOKIE! Om nom nom nom nom.

```
{cakes: 1, pies: 14, donuts: 37, brownies: 3}
```

No more cookies.

Map properties

Maps have properties just as lists do. For example, the following properties indicate (using different metrics) whether or not the map is empty:

```
inventory.isEmpty      // false
inventory.isNotEmpty   // true
inventory.length       // 4
```

You can also access the keys and values separately using the `keys` and `values` properties.

```
print(inventory.keys);
print(inventory.values);
```

When you print that out, you'll see the following:

```
(cakes, pies, donuts, brownies)
(1, 14, 37, 3)
```

Checking for key or value existence

To check whether a key is in a map, you can use the `containsKey` method:

```
print(inventory.containsKey('pies'));
// true
```

You can do the same for values using `containsValue`.

```
print(inventory.containsValue(42));
// false
```

Looping over elements of a map

Unlike lists, you can't iterate over a map using a `for-in` loop.

```
for (var item in inventory) {
  print(inventory[item]);
}
```

This will produce the following error:

```
The type 'Map<String, int>' used in the 'for' loop must
implement Iterable.
```

`Iterable` is a type that knows how to move sequentially, or *iterate*, over its elements.
`List` and `Set` both implement `Iterable`, but `Map` does not.

> **Note**: In Chapter 9 you'll learn what "implement" means.

There is a solution, though, for looping over a Map. The `keys` and `values` properties
of a map are iterables, so you can loop over them. Here's an example of iterating over
the keys:

```
for (var item in inventory.keys) {
  print(inventory[item]);
}
```

You can also use `forEach` to iterate over the elements of a map, which gives you both
the keys and the values.

```
inventory.forEach((key, value) => print('$key -> $value'));
```

And this `for` loop does the same thing:

```
for (final entry in inventory.entries) {
  print('${entry.key} -> ${entry.value}');
}
```

Running either loop gives the following result:

```
cakes -> 1
pies -> 14
donuts -> 37
brownies -> 3
```

Before going on, test your knowledge of maps with the following mini-exercises.

Mini-exercises

1. Create a map with the following keys: `name`, `profession`, `country` and `city`. For the values, add your own information.

2. You suddenly decide to move to Toronto, Canada. Programmatically update the values for `country` and `city`.

3. Iterate over the map and print all the values.

Higher order methods

There are a number of collection operations common to many programming languages, including transforming, filtering and consolidating the elements of the collection. These operations are known as **higher order methods**, because they take functions as parameters. This is a great opportunity to apply what you learned in Chapter 5 about anonymous functions.

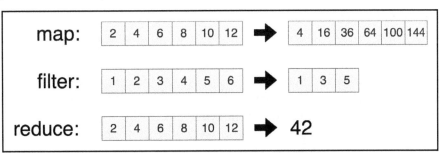

Examples of higher order methods on collections

In this section, you'll learn about the higher order methods named `map`, `where`, `reduce`, `fold` and `sort`. There are many more methods than this small sampling, though. Don't worry — you'll discover them in time.

Mapping over a collection

Mapping over a collection allows you to perform an action on each element of the collection as if you were running it through a loop. To do this, collections have a **map** method that takes an anonymous function as a parameter, and returns another collection based on what the function does to the elements.

> **Note**: The map method in this section is different than the Map data type that you studied earlier in this chapter. List, Set and Map all have a map method.

Write the following code:

```
const numbers = [1, 2, 3, 4];
final squares = numbers.map((number) => number * number);
```

The map method is very similar to forEach in that it loops through every element of the list. It takes each element and passes it in as an argument to the anonymous function. In the example above, since numbers is a list of int values, number is inferred to be of type int. The first time through the loop, number is 1, the second time through, number is 2, and so on through 4.

Inside the anonymous function body, you're allowed to do whatever you want. In the case above, you square each input value. Next is where map and forEach differ. Instead of just performing some action, map takes each resulting value and inserts it as an element in a new collection, in this case one named squares.

Print squares to see the result:

```
(1, 4, 9, 16)
```

The numbers make sense. Those are all squares of the input list. Look at the parentheses, though. Set and Map use curly braces and List uses square brackets. Hover your cursor over squares to see the type.

```
                 Iterable<int> squares
       final squares = numbers.map((number) => number * number);
```

It's actually an Iterable of int, rather than a List of int. That's why when you print squares it has parentheses rather than square brackets. If you really want a List instead of an Iterable, you can call the toList method on the result.

```
print(squares.toList());
```

Run that and now you'll have square brackets:

```
[1, 4, 9, 16]
```

It's a common mistake to forget that map produces an Iterable rather than a List, but now you know what to do. There's a similar method called toSet if you need a set instead of a list.

Filtering a collection

You can filter an iterable collection like List and Set down to another shorter collection by using the **where** method.

Add the following line below the code you already have:

```
final evens = squares.where((square) => square.isEven);
```

Like map, the where method takes an anonymous function. The function's input is also each element of the list, but unlike map, the value the function returns must be a Boolean. If the function returns true for a particular element, then that element is added to the resulting collection, but if false, then the element is excluded. Using isEven makes the condition true for even numbers, so you've filtered down squares to just the even values.

Print evens and you'll get:

```
(4, 16)
```

These are indeed even squares. As you can see by the parentheses, where also returns an Iterable.

You can use where with List and Set but not with Map, that is, unless you access the keys or values properties of Map.

Consolidating a collection

Some higher order methods take all the elements of an iterable collection and consolidate them into a single value using the function you provide. You'll learn two ways to do this.

Using reduce

One way to combine all of the elements of a list into a single value is to use the **reduce** method. You can combine the elements in any way you like, but the example below shows how to find their sum.

Given the following list of amounts, find the total value by passing in an anonymous function that adds each element to the sum of the previous ones:

```
const amounts = [199, 299, 299, 199, 499];
final total = amounts.reduce((sum, element) => sum + element);
```

The first function parameter always contains the result of the previous function call, while the second parameter contains the current element in the collection. In this example, on each iteration `sum` stores the current total while `element` is the current integer in the list.

Print `total` to see the final result of 1495.

Using fold

If you try to call `reduce` on an empty list, you'll get an error. For that reason, using **fold** may be more reliable when a collection has a possibility of containing zero elements. The `fold` method works like `reduce`, but it takes an extra parameter that provides the function with a starting value.

Here is the same result as above, but this time using `fold`:

```
const amounts = [199, 299, 299, 199, 499];
final total = amounts.fold(
  0,
  (int sum, element) => sum + element,
);
```

Notice that there are two arguments that you gave the `fold` method. The first argument `0` is the starting value. The second argument takes that `0`, feeds it to `sum`, and keeps adding to it based on the value of each `element` in the list.

Sorting a list

While `where`, `reduce` and `fold` all work equally well on lists or sets, you can only call **sort** on a list. That's because sets are by definition unordered, so it wouldn't make sense to sort them.

Calling `sort` on a list sorts the elements based on their data type.

```
final desserts = ['cookies', 'pie', 'donuts', 'brownies'];
desserts.sort();
```

Print `desserts` and you'll see the following:

```
[brownies, cookies, donuts, pie]
```

Since `desserts` holds strings, calling `sort` on the list arranges them in alphabetical order. The sorting is done in place, which means `sort` mutates the input list itself. This also means if you tried to sort a `const` list, you'd get an error.

Reversing a list

You can use `reversed` to produce a list in reverse order.

```
var dessertsReversed = desserts.reversed;
```

This produces the following result:

```
(pie, donuts, cookies, brownies)
```

Mind you, using `reversed` doesn't re-sort the list in reverse order. It just returns an `Iterable` that starts at the last element of the list and works forward. This will become clear if you look at an unsorted list:

```
final desserts = ['cookies', 'pie', 'donuts', 'brownies'];
final dessertsReversed = desserts.reversed;
print(desserts);
print(dessertsReversed);
```

Run that to see the results:

```
[cookies, pie, donuts, brownies]
(brownies, donuts, pie, cookies)
```

Neither collection is sorted, but the second one is in reverse order of the first.

This also brings up a couple of important points about naming conventions in Dart:

- You should use a commanding verb for a method that produces a side effect. The `sort()` method mutates itself, which is a side effect. Also notice the parentheses on the `sort()` method; they clearly say that this is a method, not a property, and as such, may be doing some potentially expensive work.

- In comparison, reversed is a getter property, which you recognize because it doesn't have any parentheses. This indicates that the work is lighter, usually because getters only return a value. Additionally, reversed is an adjective, not a commanding verb. That's because there are no side effects as it doesn't mutate the collection.

You won't *always* see these conventions followed, but they're general guidelines that are helpful to consider in your own naming.

> **Note**: One interesting characteristic of iterables is that they're lazy. That means they don't do any work until you ask them to. Since reversed returns an iterable, it doesn't actually reverse the elements of the collection until you try to access those elements, such as by printing the collection or converting it to a list using the toList method. Understanding this can help you put off work that doesn't need to be done yet.

Performing a custom sort

For the sort method, you can pass in a function as an argument to perform custom sorting. Say you want to sort strings by length and not alphabetically; you could give sort an anonymous function like so:

```
desserts.sort((d1, d2) => d1.length.compareTo(d2.length));
```

The names d1 and d2 aren't going to win any good naming prizes, but they fit on the page of a book better than dessertOne and dessertTwo do. The compareTo method returns –1 if the first length is shorter, 1 if it's longer, and 0 if both lengths are the same. This is all sort needs to do the custom sort.

So now desserts is sorted by the size of each string element.

```
[pie, donuts, cookies, brownies]
```

Combining higher order methods

You can chain together the higher order methods that you learned above. For example, if you wanted to take only the desserts that have a name length greater than 5 and then convert those names to uppercase, you would do it like so:

```
const desserts = ['cake', 'pie', 'donuts', 'brownies'];
final bigTallDesserts = desserts
```

```
    .where((dessert) => dessert.length > 5)
    .map((dessert) => dessert.toUpperCase());
```

Wrapping that expression onto multiple lines makes it easier to read. First you filtered the list with `where` and then mapped the resulting iterable to get the final result.

Printing `bigTallDesserts` reveals:

```
(DONUTS, BROWNIES)
```

Mini-exercises

Given the following exam scores:

```
final scores = [89, 77, 46, 93, 82, 67, 32, 88];
```

1. Use `sort` to find the highest and lowest grades.

2. Use `where` to find all the B grades, that is, all the scores between 80 and 90.

When to use lists, sets or maps

Congratulations on making it through another chapter! You've made a ton of progress. This chapter will leave you with some advice about when to use which type of collection. Each type has its strengths.

- Choose **lists** if order matters. Try to insert at the end of lists wherever possible to keep things running smoothly. And be aware that searching can be slow with big collections.

- Choose **sets** if you are only concerned with whether something is in the collection or not. This is faster than searching a list.

- Choose **maps** if you frequently need to search for a value by a key. Searching by key is also fast.

Challenges

Before moving on, here are some challenges to test your knowledge of collections. It's best if you try to solve them yourself, but solutions are available with the supplementary materials for this book if you get stuck.

Challenge 1: A unique request

Write a function that takes a paragraph of text and returns a collection of unique String characters that the text contains.

Challenge 2: Counting on you

Repeat Challenge 1, but this time have the function return a collection that contains the frequency, or count, of every unique character.

Challenge 3: Mapping users

Create a class called User with properties for id and name. Make a List with three users, specifying any appropriate names and IDs you like. Then write a function that converts your user list to a list of maps whose keys are id and name.

Key points

- Lists store an ordered collection of elements.

- Sets store an unordered collection of unique elements.

- Maps store a collection of key-value pairs.

- The elements of a collection are mutable by default.

- The spread operator (...) allows you to expand one collection inside another collection.

- Collection `if` and `for` can be used to dynamically create the content of a list or set.

- You can iterate over any collection, but for a map you need to iterate over the keys or values if you use a `for-in` loop.

- Higher order methods take a function as a parameter and act on the elements of a collection.

- The `map` method, not to be confused with the `Map` type, performs an operation on each element of a collection and returns the results as an `Iterable`.

- The `where` method filters an iterable collection based on a condition.

- The `reduce` and `fold` methods consolidate a collection down to a single value.

- The `sort` method sorts a list in place according to its data type.

Where to go from here?

As jam-packed as this chapter was, it still didn't include all there is to know about collections! For example, another collection type that Dart has is **Queue**, which is a **first-in, first-out** data structure. This chapter also didn't go into great detail about iterables. To explore more about collections and their methods in Dart, you can browse the contents of the `dart:collection` library.

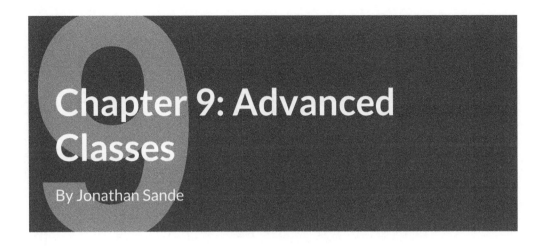

Chapter 9: Advanced Classes

By Jonathan Sande

Chapter 6 covered a lot of the foundational elements of classes, but now it's time to extend that knowledge. Object-oriented programming has captured developers' imaginations for decades. Just as the name class is inspired by biological notation, the true beauty of object-oriented programming is how you're able to elegantly build connective tissue between your classes. In this chapter you'll learn to use tools such as inheritance, interfaces, mixins and extension methods to move beyond simple coding and enter a world of software design.

Extending classes

In many situations, you'll need to create a hierarchy of classes that share some base functionality. You can create your own hierarchies by **extending classes**. This is also called **inheritance**, because the classes form a tree in which **child classes** inherit from **parent classes**. The parent and child classes are also called **super classes** and **subclasses** respectively. The Object class is the top superclass for all non-nullable types in Dart. All other classes (except Null) are subclasses of Object.

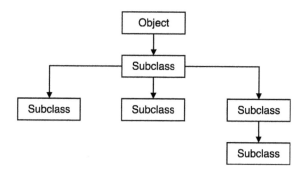

Note: Although there is no named top type in Dart, since all non-nullable Dart types derive from the Object type and Object itself is a subtype of the nullable Object? type, Object? can be considered in practice to be the root of the type system.

Creating your first subclass

To see how inheritance works, you'll create your own hierarchy of classes. In a little while, you'll make a Student class which needs grades, so first make a Grade enum:

```
enum Grade { A, B, C, D, F }
```

Creating similar classes

Next create two classes named Person and Student.

Here's Person:

```
class Person {
  Person(this.givenName, this.surname);

  String givenName;
  String surname;
  String get fullName => '$givenName $surname';

  @override
  String toString() => fullName;
}
```

And this is `Student`:

```
class Student {
  Student(this.givenName, this.surname);

  String givenName;
  String surname;
  var grades = <Grade>[];
  String get fullName => '$givenName $surname';

  @override
  String toString() => fullName;
}
```

Naturally, the `Person` and `Student` classes are very similar, since students are in fact persons. The only difference at the moment is that a `Student` will have a list of grades.

Subclassing to remove code duplication

You can remove the duplication between `Student` and `Person` by making `Student` **extend** `Person`. You do so by adding extends `Person` after the class name, and removing everything but the `Student` constructor and the `grades` list.

Replace the `Student` class with the following code:

```
class Student extends Person {
  Student(String givenName, String surname)
    : super(givenName, surname);

  var grades = <Grade>[];
}
```

There are a few points to pay attention to:

- The constructor parameter names don't refer to `this` anymore. Whenever you see the keyword `this`, you should remember that `this` refers to the current object, which in this case would be an instance of the `Student` class. Since `Student` no longer contains the field names `givenName` and `surname`, using `this.givenName` or `this.surname` would have nothing to reference.

- In contrast to `this`, the super keyword is used to refer one level up the hierarchy. Similar to the forwarding constructor that you learned about in Chapter 6, using `super(givenName, surname)` passes the constructor parameters on to another constructor. However, since you're using super instead of `this`, you're forwarding the parameters to the parent class's constructor, that is, to the constructor of `Person`.

Calling super last in an initializer list

As a quick side note, if you use an initializer list, the call to super always goes last, that is, after assert statements and initializers. You can see the order in the following example:

```
class SomeChild extends SomeParent {

  SomeChild(double height)
      : assert(height != 0),  // assert
        _height = height,     // initializer
        super();              // super

  final double _height;
}
```

In this example, calling super() is actually unnecessary, because Dart always calls the default constructor for the super class if there are no arguments to pass. The reason that you or Dart always need to make the super call is to ensure that all of the field values have finished initializing.

Using the classes

OK, back to the primary example. Create Person and Student objects like so:

```
final jon = Person('Jon', 'Snow');
final jane = Student('Jane', 'Snow');
print(jon.fullName);
print(jane.fullName);
```

Run that and observe that both have full names:

```
Jon Snow
Jane Snow
```

The fullName for Student is coming from the Person class.

If you have a grade, you can only add that grade to the Student and not to the Person, because only the Student has grades. Add the following two lines to main:

```
final historyGrade = Grade.B;
jane.grades.add(historyGrade);
```

The student jane now has one grade in the grades list.

Overriding parent methods

Suppose you want the student's full name to print out differently than the default way it's printed in Person. You can do so by **overriding** the fullName getter. Add the following two lines to the bottom of the Student class:

```
@override
String get fullName => '$surname, $givenName';
```

You've seen the @override annotation before in this book with the toString method. While using @override is technically optional in Dart, it does help in that the compiler will give you an error if you think you're overriding something that doesn't actually exist in the parent class.

Run the code now and you'll see the student's full name printed differently than the parent's.

```
Jon Snow
Snow, Jane
```

Calling super from an overridden method

As another aside, sometimes you override methods of the parent class because you want to *add* functionality, rather than replace it, as you did above. In that case, you usually make a call to super either at the beginning or end of the overridden method.

Have a look at the following example:

```
class SomeParent {
  void doSomeWork() {
    print('parent working');
  }
}

class SomeChild extends SomeParent {
  @override
  void doSomeWork() {
    super.doSomeWork();
    print('child doing some other work');
  }
}
```

Since `doSomeWork` in the child class makes a call to `super.doSomeWork`, both the parent and the child methods run. So if you were to call the child method like so:

```
final child = SomeChild();
child.doSomeWork();
```

You would see the following result:

```
parent working
child doing some other work
```

The parent method's work was done first, since you had the `super` call at the *beginning* of the overridden method in the child. If you wanted to do the child method's work first, though, you would put the `super` call at the *end* of the method, like so:

```
@override
void doSomeWork() {
  print('child doing some other work');
  super.doSomeWork();
}
```

Multi-level hierarchy

Back to the primary example again. Add more than one level to your class hierarchy by defining a class that extends from `Student`.

```
class SchoolBandMember extends Student {
  SchoolBandMember(String givenName, String surname)
    : super(givenName, surname);
  static const minimumPracticeTime = 2;
}
```

`SchoolBandMember` is a `Student` that has a `minimumPracticeTime`. The `SchoolBandMember` constructor calls the `Student` constructor with the `super` keyword. The `Student` constructor will, in turn, call the `Person` constructor.

Sibling classes

Create a sibling class to `SchoolBandMember` named `StudentAthlete` that also derives from `Student`.

```
class StudentAthlete extends Student {
  StudentAthlete(String givenName, String surname)
    : super(givenName, surname);
```

```
    bool get isEligible =>
      grades.every((grade) => grade != Grade.F);
  }
```

In order to remain eligible for athletics, a student athlete has an isEligible getter that makes sure the athlete has not failed any classes. The higher order method every on the grades list only returns true if every element of the list passes the given condition, which, in this case, means that none of the grades are F.

So now you can create band members and athletes.

```
final jessie = SchoolBandMember('Jessie', 'Jones');
final marty = StudentAthlete('Marty', 'McFly');
```

Visualizing the hierarchy

Here's what your class hierarchy looks like now:

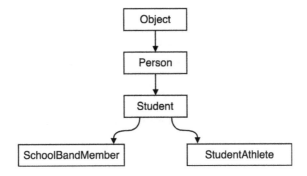

You see that SchoolBandMember and StudentAthlete are both students, and all students are also persons.

Type inference in a mixed list

Since Jane, Jessie and Marty are all students, you can put them into a list.

```
final students = [jane, jessie, marty];
```

Recall that jane is a Student, jessie is a SchoolBandMember and marty is a StudentAthlete. Since they are all different types, what type is the list?

Hover your cursor over students to find out.

```
List<Student> students
final students = [jane, jessie, marty];
```

You can see that Dart has inferred the type of the list to be List<Student>. Dart used the most specific common ancestor as the type for the list. It couldn't use SchoolBandMember or StudentAthlete, since that doesn't hold true for all elements of the list.

Checking an object's type at runtime

You can use the is and is! keywords to check whether a given object is or is not within the direct hierarchy of a class. Write the following code:

```
print(jessie is Object);
print(jessie is Person);
print(jessie is Student);
print(jessie is SchoolBandMember);
print(jessie is! StudentAthlete);
```

Knowing that jessie is a SchoolBandMember, first guess what Dart will show, and then run the code to see if you were right.

Ready? All five will print true, since jessie is SchoolBandMember, which is a subclass of Student, which is a subclass of Person, which is a subclass of Object. The only type that jessie is not, is StudentAthlete — which you confirmed by using the is! keyword.

> **Note**: The exclamation mark at the end of is! has nothing to do with the null assignment operator from null safety. It just means *not*.

Having an object be able to take multiple forms is known as **polymorphism**. This is a key part of object-oriented programming. You'll learn to make polymorphic classes in an even more sophisticated way with abstract classes in just a bit.

First, though, a word of caution.

Prefer composition over inheritance

Now that you know about inheritance, you may feel ready to conquer the world. You can model anything as a hierarchy. Experience, though, will teach you that deep hierarchies are not always the best choice.

You may have already noticed this fact in the code above. For example, when you're overriding a method, do you need to call `super`? And if you do, should you call `super` at the beginning of the method, or at the end? Often the only way to know is to check the source code of the parent class. Jumping back and forth between levels of the hierarchy can make coding difficult.

Another problem with hierarchies is that they're tightly bound together. Changes to a parent class can break a child class. For example, say that you wanted to "fix" the `Person` class by removing `givenName` and replacing it with `firstName` and `middleName`.

Doing this would also require you to update, or refactor, all of the code that uses the subclasses as well. Even if you didn't remove `givenName`, but simply added `middleName`, users of classes like `StudentBandMember` would be affected without realizing it.

Tight coupling isn't the only problem. What if Jessie, who is a school band member, also decides to become an athlete? Do you make another class called `SchoolBandMemberAndStudentAthlete`? What if she joins the student union, too? Obviously, things could get out of hand quickly.

This has led many people to say, **prefer composition over inheritance**. The phrase means that, when appropriate, you should *add* behavior to a class rather than share behavior with an ancestor. It's more of a focus on what an object *has*, rather than what an object *is*. For example, you could flatten the hierarchy for `Student` by giving the student a list of roles, like so:

```
class Student {
  List<Role>? roles;
}
```

When you create a student, you could pass in the roles as a constructor parameter. This would also let you add and remove roles later. Of course, since Dart doesn't come with the `Role` type, you'd have to define it yourself. You'd need to make `Role` abstract enough so that a role could be a band member, an athlete or a student union member. You'll learn about making abstract classes like this in the next section of the chapter.

All this talk of composition isn't to say that inheritance is *always* bad. It might make sense to still have `Student` extend `Person`. Inheritance can be good when a subclass needs *all* of the behavior of its parent. However, when you only need some of that behavior, you should consider passing in the behavior as a parameter, or perhaps even using a mixin, which you'll learn about later in this chapter.

> **Note**: The whole Flutter framework is organized around the idea of composition. You build your UI as a tree of widgets, where each widget *does* one simple thing and *has* zero or more child widgets that also do one simple thing. This type of architecture generally makes it easier to understand the purpose of a class.

Mini-exercises

1. Create a class named `Fruit` with a `String` field named `color` and a method named `describeColor`, which uses `color` to print a message.

2. Create a subclass of `Fruit` named `Melon` and then create two `Melon` subclasses named `Watermelon` and `Cantaloupe`.

3. Override `describeColor` in the `Watermelon` class to vary the output.

Abstract classes

The classes and subclasses you created in the last section were **concrete classes**. It's not that they're made of cement; it just means that you can make actual objects out of them. That's in contrast to **abstract classes**, from which you can't make objects.

"What's the use of a class you can't make an object out of?" asks the pragmatist. "What are the use of ideas?" answers the philosopher. You deal with abstract concepts all the time, and you don't think about them at all.

Have you ever seen an animal? "Uh, are you seriously asking me that?" you answer. The question isn't "have you ever seen a chicken or a platypus or a mouse." Have you ever seen a generic animal, devoid of all features that are relevant to only one kind of animal — just the essence of "animal" itself? What would that even look like? It can't have four legs because ducks are animals and they have two legs. It can't have hair because rattlesnakes are animals and they don't have hair. Worms are animals, too, right? So there go the eyes and bones.

No one has seen an "animal" in the abstract sense, but everybody has seen concrete instances of things that fit the abstract animal category. Humans are good at generalizing and categorizing the observations they make, and honestly, these abstract ideas are very useful. They allow you to make short statements like "I saw a lot of animals at the zoo" instead of "I saw a lion, an elephant, a lemur, a shark, …"

The same thing applies in object oriented programming. After making lots of concrete classes, you begin to notice patterns and more generalized characteristics of the classes you're writing. So when you come to the point of just wanting to describe the general characteristics and behavior of a class without specifying the exact way that class is implemented, you're ready to write abstract classes. Don't be put off by the word "abstract". It's no more difficult than the idea of an animal.

Creating your own abstract classes

Have a go at working this out in Dart now. Without venturing too far into the fringes of how taxonomists make their decisions, create the following `Animal` class:

```dart
abstract class Animal {
  bool isAlive = true;
  void eat();
  void move();

  @override
  String toString() {
    return "I'm a $runtimeType";
  }
}
```

Here are a few important points about that code:

- The way you define an abstract class in Dart is to put the `abstract` keyword before `class`.

- In addition to the class itself being abstract, `Animal` also has two abstract methods: `eat` and `move`. You know they're abstract because they don't have curly braces; they just end with a semicolon.

- These abstract methods describe behavior that a subclass must implement but don't tell *how* to implement. That's up to the subclass. Leaving implementation details up to the subclass is a good thing because there are such a variety of ways to eat and move throughout the animal kingdom, so it would be almost impossible for `Animal` to specify anything meaningful here.

- Note that just because a class is abstract doesn't mean that it can't have concrete methods or data. You can see that `Animal` has a concrete `isAlive` field, with a default value of `true`. `Animal` also has a concrete implementation of the `toString` method, which belongs to the `Object` superclass. The `runtimeType` property also comes from `Object` and gives the object type at runtime.

Can't instantiate abstract classes

As mentioned, you can't create an instance of an abstract class. See for yourself by writing the following line:

```
final animal = Animal();
```

You'll see the following error:

```
Abstract classes can't be instantiated.
Try creating an instance of a concrete subtype.
```

Isn't that good advice! That's what you're going to do next.

Concrete subclass

Create a concrete `Platypus` now. Stop thinking about cement. Just add the following empty class to your IDE below your `Animal` class:

```
class Platypus extends Animal {}
```

Immediately you'll notice the wavy red line:

```
class Platypus extends Animal {}
```

That's not because you spelled platypus wrong. It really does have a *y*. Rather, the error is because when you extend an abstract class, you must provide an implementation of any abstract methods, which in this case are `eat` and `move`.

Adding the missing methods

You could write the methods yourself, but VS Code gives you a shortcut. Put your cursor on `Platypus` and press `Command+.` on a Mac or `Control+.` on a PC. You'll see the following pop-up:

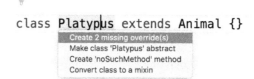

To quickly add the missing methods, choose **Create 2 missing override(s)**.

This will give you the following code:

```
class Platypus extends Animal {
  @override
  void eat() {
    // TODO: implement eat
  }

  @override
  void move() {
    // TODO: implement move
  }
}
```

Starting a comment with TODO: is a common way to mark parts of your code where you need to do more work. Later, you can search your entire project in VS Code for the remaining TODOs by pressing **Command+Shift+F** on a Mac or **Control+Shift+F** on a PC and writing "TODO" in the search box. You're going to complete these TODOs right now, though.

Filling in the TODOs

Since this is a concrete class, it needs to provide the actual implementation of the eat and move methods. In the eat method body, add the following line:

```
print('Munch munch');
```

A platypus may not have teeth, but it should still be able to munch.

In the move method add:

```
print('Glide glide');
```

As was true with subclassing normal classes, abstract class subclasses can also have their own unique methods. Add the following method to Platypus:

```
void layEggs() {
  print('Plop plop');
}
```

Readers who are well-acquainted with how platypuses (Or is it platypi?) eat, swim and give birth can make additional word suggestions for the next edition of this book.

Testing the results

Test your code out now in `main`:

```
final platypus = Platypus();
print(platypus.isAlive);
platypus.eat();
platypus.move();
platypus.layEggs();
print(platypus);
```

Run the code to see the following:

```
true
Munch munch
Glide glide
Plop plop
I'm a Platypus
```

Look at what this tells you:

- A concrete class has access to concrete data, like `isAlive`, from its abstract parent class.

- Dart recognized that the runtime type was `Platypus`, even though `runtimeType` comes from `Object`, and was accessed in the `toString` method of `Animal`.

Treating concrete classes as abstract

There is one more interesting thing to do before moving on. In the line where you declared `platypus`, hover your cursor over the variable name:

```
           Platypus platypus
final platypus = Platypus();
```

Dart infers `platypus` to be of type `Platypus`. That's normal, but here's the interesting part. Replace that line with the following one, adding the `Animal` type annotation:

```
Animal platypus = Platypus();
```

Hover your cursor over platypus again:

```
Animal platypus
Animal platypus = Platypus();
```

Now Dart sees `platypus` as merely an `Animal` with no more special ability to lay eggs. Comment out the line calling the `layEggs` method:

```
// platypus.layEggs();
```

Run the code again paying special attention to the `print(platypus)` results:

```
I'm a Platypus
```

So at compile time, Dart treats `platypus` like an `Animal` even though at runtime Dart knows it's a `Platypus`. This is useful when you don't care about about the concrete implementation of an abstract class, but you only care that it's an `Animal` with `Animal` characteristics.

Now, you're probably thinking, "Making animal classes is very cute and all, but how does this help me save data on the awesome new social media app I'm making?" That's where interfaces come in.

Interfaces

Interfaces are similar to abstract classes in that they let you define the behavior you expect for all classes that implement the interface. They're a means of hiding the implementation details of the concrete classes from the rest of your code. Why is that important? To answer that question it's helpful to understand a little about architecture. Not the Taj Mahal kind of architecture, software architecture.

Software architecture

When you're building an app, your goal should be to keep core business logic separate from infrastructure like the UI, database, network and third-party packages. Why? The core business logic doesn't change frequently, while the infrastructure often does. Mixing unstable code with stable would cause the stable code to become unstable.

Note: **Business logic**, which is sometimes called **business rules** or **domain logic**, refers to the essence of what your app does. The business logic of a calculator app would be the mathematical calculations themselves. Those calculations don't depend on what your UI looks like or how you store the answers.

The following image shows an idealized app with the stable business logic in the middle and the more volatile infrastructure parts surrounding it:

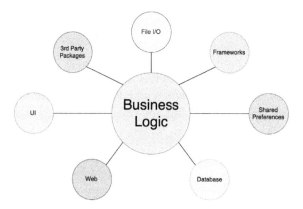

The UI shouldn't communicate directly with the web. You also shouldn't scatter direct calls to the database across your app. Everything goes through the central business logic. In addition to that, the business logic shouldn't know any implementation details about the infrastructure.

This gives you a plug-in style architecture, where you can swap one database framework for another and the rest of the app won't even know anything changed. You could replace your mobile UI with a desktop UI, and the rest of the app wouldn't care. This is useful for building scalable, maintainable and testable apps.

Communication rules

Here's where interfaces come in. An **interface** is a description of how communication will be managed between two parties. A phone number is a type of interface. If you want to call your friend, you have to dial your friend's phone number. Dialing a different number won't work. Another word for interface is **protocol**, as in Internet Protocol or Hypertext Transfer Protocol. Those protocols are the rules for how communication happens among the users of the protocol.

When you create an interface in Dart, you define the rules for how one part of your codebase will communicate with another part. As long as both parts follow the interface rules, each part can change independently of the other. This makes your app much more manageable. In team settings, interfaces also allow different people to work on different parts of the codebase without worrying that they're going to mess up someone else's code.

Separating business logic from infrastructure

In the image below, you can see the interface is between the business logic and the code for accessing the database.

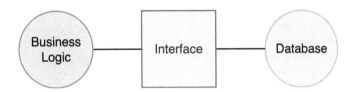

The business logic doesn't know anything about the database. It's just talking to the interface. That means you could even swap out the database for a completely different form of storage like cloud storage or file storage. The business logic doesn't care.

There's a famous adage related to this that goes, **code against interfaces, not implementations**. You define an interface, and then you code your app to use that interface only. While you must implement the interface with concrete classes, the rest of your app shouldn't know anything about those concrete classes, only the interface.

Creating an interface

There's no `interface` keyword in Dart. Instead, you can use any class as an interface. Since only the field and method names are important, most interfaces are made from abstract classes that contain no logic.

Say you want to make a weather app, and your business logic needs to get the current temperature in some city. Since those are the requirements, your Dart interface class would look like this:

```
abstract class DataRepository {
  double? fetchTemperature(String city);
}
```

Note that **repository** is a common term to call an interface that hides the details of how data is stored and retrieved. Also, the reason the result of fetchTemperature is nullable is that someone might ask for the temperature in a city that doesn't exist.

Implementing the interface

The Dart class above was just a normal abstract class, like the one you made earlier. However, when creating a concrete class to implement the interface, you must use the implements keyword instead of the extends keyword.

Add the following concrete class:

```
class FakeWebServer implements DataRepository {
  @override
  double? fetchTemperature(String city) {
    return 42.0;
  }
}
```

Here are a couple of points to note:

- Besides the benefits mentioned previously, another great advantage of using an interface is that you can create mock implementations to temporarily replace real implementations. In the FakeWebServer class, you are simply returning a random number instead of going to all the work of contacting a real server. This allows you to have a "working" app until you can get around to writing the code to contact the web server. This is also useful when you're testing your code and you don't want to wait for a real connection to the server.

- Speaking of waiting for a web server, a real interface would return a type of Future<double?> instead of returning double? directly. However, you haven't read Chapter 10 about asynchronous programming yet, so this example omits the Future part.

Using the interface

How do you use the interface on the business logic side? Remember that you can't instantiate an abstract class, so this won't work:

```
final repository = DataRepository();
```

You could potentially use the `FakeWebServer` implementation directly like so:

```
final DataRepository repository = FakeWebServer();
final temperature = repository.fetchTemperature('Berlin');
```

But this defeats the whole point of trying to keep the implementation details separate from the business logic. When you get around to swapping out the `FakeWebServer` with another class, you'll have to go back and make updates at every place in your business logic that mentions it.

Adding a factory constructor

Do you remember factory constructors from Chapter 6? If you do, you'll recall that factory constructors can return subclasses. Add the following line to your interface class:

```
factory DataRepository() => FakeWebServer();
```

Your interface should look like this now:

```
abstract class DataRepository {
  factory DataRepository() => FakeWebServer();
  double? fetchTemperature(String city);
}
```

Since `FakeWebServer` is a subclass of `DataRepository`, the factory constructor is allowed to return it. The neat trick is that by using an unnamed constructor for the factory, you can make it look like it's possible to instantiate the class now.

Write the following in `main`:

```
final repository = DataRepository();
final temperature = repository.fetchTemperature('Manila');
```

Ah, now your code on this side has no idea that that repository is actually `FakeWebServer`. When it comes time to swap in the real implementation, you only need to update the subclass returned by the factory constructor in the `DataRepository` interface.

> **Note:** In the code above, you used a factory to return the concrete implementation of the interface. There are other options, though. Do a search for **service locators**, of which the get_it package is a good example, and **dependency injection** to learn more about this topic.

Interfaces and the Dart SDK

If you browse the Dart source code, which you can do by Command or Control-clicking Dart class names like `int` or `List` or `String`, you'll see that Dart makes heavy use of interfaces to define its API. That allows the Dart team to change the implementation details without affecting developers. The only time developers are affected is when the interface changes.

This concept is key to the flexibility that Dart has as a language. The Dart VM implements the interface one way and gives you the ability to hot-reload your Flutter apps. The `dart compile js` tool implements the interface using JavaScript and gives you the ability to run your code on the web. The `dart compile exe` tool implements the interface on Windows or Linux or Mac to let you run your code on those platforms.

The implementation details are different for every platform, but you don't have to worry about that, because your code will only talk to the interface, not to the platform. Are you starting to see how powerful interfaces can be?

Extending vs implementing

There are a couple of differences between `extends` and `implements`. Dart only allows you to extend a single superclass. This is known as **single inheritance**, in contrast with other languages that allow **multiple inheritance**.

So the following is not allowed in Dart:

```
class MySubclass extends OneClass, AnotherClass {} // Not OK
```

However, you can implement more than one interface:

```
class MyClass implements OneClass, AnotherClass {} // OK
```

You can also combine `extends` and `implements`:

```
class MySubclass extends OneClass implements AnotherClass {}
```

But what's the difference between just extending or implementing? That is, how are these two lines different?

```
class SomeClass extends AnotherClass {}
class SomeClass implements AnotherClass {}
```

When you extend `AnotherClass`, `SomeClass` has access to any logic or variables in `AnotherClass`. However, if `SomeClass` *implements* `AnotherClass`, `SomeClass` must provide its own version of all methods and variables in `AnotherClass`.

Example of extending

Assume `AnotherClass` looks like the following:

```
class AnotherClass {
  int myField = 42;
  void myMethod() => print(myField);
}
```

You can extend it like this with no issue:

```
class SomeClass extends AnotherClass {}
```

Check that `SomeClass` objects have access to `AnotherClass` data and methods:

```
final someClass = SomeClass();
print(someClass.myField);      // 42
someClass.myMethod();          // 42
```

Run that and you'll see 42 printed twice.

Example of implementing

Using `implements` in the same way doesn't work:

```
class SomeClass implements AnotherClass {} // Not OK
```

The `implements` keyword tells Dart that you only want the field types and method signatures. You'll provide the concrete implementation details for everything yourself. How you implement it is up to you, as demonstrated in the following example:

```
class SomeClass implements AnotherClass {
  @override
  int myField = 0;

  @override
  void myMethod() => print('Hello');
}
```

Test that code again as before:

```
final someClass = SomeClass();
print(someClass.myField);      // 0
someClass.myMethod();          // Hello
```

This time you see your custom implementation results in 0 and Hello.

Mini-exercises

1. Create an interface called Bottle and add a method to it called open.

2. Create a concrete class called SodaBottle that implements Bottle and prints "Fizz fizz" when open is called.

3. Add a factory constructor to Bottle that returns a SodaBottle instance.

4. Instantiate SodaBottle by using the Bottle factory constructor and call open on the object.

Mixins

Mixins are an interesting feature of Dart that you might not be familiar with, even if you know other programming languages. They're a way to reuse methods or variables among otherwise unrelated classes.

> **Note**: For you Swift developers, Dart mixins work like protocol extensions.

Before showing you what mixins look like, first you'll take a look at why you need them.

Problems with extending and implementing

Think back to the Animal examples again. Say you've got a bunch of birds, so you're carefully planning an abstract class to represent them. Here's what you come up with:

```
abstract class Bird {
  void fly();
  void layEggs();
}
```

tion only.1

```

"It's looking good!" you think. "I'm getting the hang of this." So you try it out on Robin:

```
class Robin extends Bird {
  @override
  void fly() {
    print('Swoosh swoosh');
  }

  @override
  void layEggs() {
    print('Plop plop');
  }
}
```

"Perfect!" You smile contentedly at your handiwork.

Then you hear a sound behind you.

"Munch, munch. Glide, glide. Plop, plop. I'm a platypus."

Oh. Right. The platypus.

Your layEggs code for Robin is exactly the same as it is for Platypus. That means you're duplicating code, which violates the DRY principle. If there are any future changes to layEggs, you'll have to remember to change both instances. Consider your options:

1. Platypus can't extend Bird or Robin, because platypi can't fly.

2. Birds probably shouldn't extend Platypus, because who knows when you're going to add the stingWithVenomSpur method?

3. You could create an EggLayer class and have Bird and Platypus both extend that. But then what about flying? Make a Flyer class, too? Dart only allows you to extend one class, so that won't work.

4. You could have birds implement EggLayer and Flyer while Platypus implements only EggLayer. But then you're back to code duplication, since implementing requires you to supply the implementation code for every class.

The solution? Mixins!
```

Mixing in code

To make a **mixin**, you take whatever concrete code you want to share with different classes, and package it in its own special mixin class.

Write the following two mixins:

```
mixin EggLayer {
  void layEggs() {
    print('Plop plop');
  }
}

mixin Flyer {
  void fly() {
    print('Swoosh swoosh');
  }
}
```

The mixin keyword indicates that these classes can *only* be used as mixins. You can use any class as a mixin, though, so if you wanted to use EggLayer as a normal class, then just replace the mixin keyword with class or abstract class. In fact, the mixin keyword is a fairly new addition to Dart, so you may still see legacy code that just uses regular classes as mixins even though those classes aren't needed as standalone classes.

Now refactor Robin as follows, using the with keyword to identify the mixins:

```
class Robin extends Bird with EggLayer, Flyer {}
```

There are two mixins, so you separate them with a comma. Since those two mixins contain all the code that Bird needs, the class body is now empty.

Refactor Platypus as well:

```
class Platypus extends Animal with EggLayer {
  @override
  void eat() {
    print('Munch munch');
  }

  @override
  void move() {
    print('Glide glide');
  }
}
```

The `layEggs` logic has moved to the mixin. Now both `Robin` and `Platypus` share the code that the `EggLayer` mixin contains. Just to make sure it works, run the following code:

```
final platypus = Platypus();
final robin = Robin();
platypus.layEggs();
robin.layEggs();
```

Four plops, and all is well.

Mini-exercises

1. Create a class called `Calculator` with a method called `sum` that prints the sum of any two integers you give it.

2. Extract the logic in `sum` to a mixin called `Adder`.

3. Use the mixin in `Calculator`.

Extension methods

Up to this point in the chapter, you've been writing your own classes and methods. Often, though, you use other people's classes when you're programming. Those classes may be part of a core Dart library, or they may be from packages that you got off Pub. In either case, you don't have the ability to modify them at will.

However, Dart has a feature called **extension methods** that allow you to add functionality to existing classes. Even though they're called extension *methods*, you can also add other members like getters, setters or even operators.

Extension syntax

To make an extension, you use the following syntax:

```
extension on SomeClass {
  // your custom code
}
```

This should be located at the top-level in a file; that is, not inside another class or function. Replace `SomeClass` with whatever class you want to add extra functionality to.

You may give the extension itself a name if you like. In that case the syntax is as follows:

```
extension YourExtensionName on ClassName {
  // your custom code
}
```

You can use whatever name you like in place of YourExtensionName. The name is only used to show or hide the extension when importing it in another library.

Have a look at a few of the following examples to see how extension methods work.

String extension example

Did you ever make secret codes when you were a kid, like a=1, b=2, c=3, and so on? For this example, you're going to make an extension that will convert a string into a secret coded message. Then you'll add another extension method to decode it.

In this secret code, each letter will be bumped up to the next one. So **a** will be **b**, **b** will be **c**, and so on. To accomplish that you'll increase the Unicode value of each code point in the input string by 1. If the original message were "abc", the encoded message should be "bcd".

Solving in the normal way

First, solve the problem as you would with a normal function.

```
String encode(String input) {
  final output = StringBuffer();
  for (final codePoint in input.runes) {
    output.writeCharCode(codePoint + 1);
  }
  return output.toString();
}
```

This function uses a StringBuffer for efficient string manipulation. A normal String is immutable, but a StringBuffer is mutable. That means your function doesn't have to create a new string every time you append a character. You loop through each Unicode code point and increment it by 1 before writing it to output. Finally, you convert the StringBuffer back to a regular String and return it.

Test it out:

```
final original = 'abc';
final secret = encode(original);
print(secret);
```

The result is bcd. It works!

Converting to an extension

The next step is to convert the encode function above to an extension so that you can use it like so:

```
final secret = 'abc'.encoded;
```

Since this extension won't mutate the original string itself, remember the naming convention of using an adjective rather than a commanding verb. That's the reason for choosing encoded, rather than encode, for the extension name.

Add the following code somewhere outside the main method:

```
extension on String {
  String get encoded {
    final output = StringBuffer();
    for (final codePoint in runes) {
      output.writeCharCode(codePoint + 1);
    }
    return output.toString();
  }
}
```

Look at what's changed here:

- The keywords extension on are what make this an extension. You can add whatever you want inside the body. It's as if String were your own class now.

- Rather than making a normal method, you can use a getter method. This makes it so that you can call the extension using encoded, without the parentheses, rather than encoded().

- Since you're inside String already, there's no need to pass input as an argument. If you need a reference to the string object, you can use the this keyword. Thus, instead of input.runes, you could write this.runes. However, this is unnecessary and you can directly access runes. Remember that runes is a member of String and you're inside String.

Check that the extension works:

```
final secret = 'abc'.encoded;
print(secret);
```

You should see bcd as the output. Nice! It still works.

Adding a decode extension

Add the decoded method inside the body of the String extension as well:

```
String get decoded {
  final output = StringBuffer();
  for (final codePoint in runes) {
    output.writeCharCode(codePoint - 1);
  }
  return output.toString();
}
```

If you compare this to the encoded method, though, there's a lot of code duplication. Whenever you see code duplication, you should think about how to make it DRY.

Refactoring to remove code duplication

Refactor your String extension by replacing the entire extension with the following:

```
extension on String {
  String get encoded {
    return _code(1);
  }
  String get decoded {
    return _code(-1);
  }
  String _code(int step) {
    final output = StringBuffer();
    for (final codePoint in runes) {
      output.writeCharCode(codePoint + step);
    }
    return output.toString();
  }
}
```

Now the private _code method factors out all of the common parts of encoded and decoded. That's better.

Testing the results

To make sure that everything works, test both methods like so:

```
final original = 'I like extensions!';
final secret = original.encoded;
final revealed = secret.decoded;
print(secret);
print(revealed);
```

This will display the following encoded and decoded messages:

```
J!mjlf!fyufotjpot"
I like extensions!
```

Great! Now you can amuse your friends by giving them encoded messages. They're actually a lot of fun to solve.

int extension example

Here's an example for an extension on `int`.

```
extension on int {
  int get cubed {
    return this * this * this;
  }
}
```

Notice the use of `this` to get a reference to the `int` object, which will be 5 in the example below.

You use the extension like so:

```
print(5.cubed);
```

The answer is 125.

Enum extension example

Dart enums, which you learned about in Chapter 4, are pretty basic in themselves. However, with the power of extensions, you can do much more with them.

First define an enum like so:

```
enum ProgrammingLanguage { dart, swift, javaScript }
```

Normally you wouldn't be able to perform any internal logic on those enum values, but you can by adding the following extension on `ProgrammingLanguage`:

```
extension on ProgrammingLanguage {
  bool get isStronglyTyped {
    switch (this) {
      case ProgrammingLanguage.dart:
      case ProgrammingLanguage.swift:
        return true;
      case ProgrammingLanguage.javaScript:
        return false;
      default:
        throw Exception('Unknown Programming Language $this');
    }
  }
}
```

Now you can check at runtime whether a particular language is strongly typed or not:

```
final language = ProgrammingLanguage.dart;
print(language.isStronglyTyped);
```

Run that and you'll see `true` printed to the console.

As you can see, you can do a lot with extensions. Although they can be very powerful, extensions by definition add non-standard behavior, and this can make it harder for other developers to understand your code. Use extensions when they make sense, but try not to overuse them.

Challenges

Before moving on, here are some challenges to test your knowledge of advanced classes. It's best if you try to solve them yourself, but solutions are available with the supplementary materials for this book if you get stuck.

Challenge 1: Heavy monotremes

Dart has a class named Comparable, which is used by the the sort method of List to sort its elements. Add a weight field to the Platypus class you made in this lesson. Then make Platypus implement Comparable so that when you have a list of Platypus objects, calling sort on the list will sort them by weight.

Challenge 2: Fake notes

Design an interface to sit between the business logic of your note-taking app and a SQL database. After that, implement a fake database class that will return mock data.

Challenge 3: Time to code

Dart has a Duration class for expressing lengths of time. Make an extension on int so that you can express a duration like so:

```
final timeRemaining = 3.minutes;
```

Key points

- A subclass has access to the data and methods of its parent class.

- You can create a subclass of another class by using the `extends` keyword.

- A subclass can override its parent's methods or properties to provide custom behavior.

- Dart only allows single inheritance on its classes.

- Abstract classes define class members and may or may not contain concrete logic.

- Abstract classes can't be instantiated.

- One rule of clean architecture is to separate business logic from infrastructure logic like the UI, storage, third-party packages and the network.

- Interfaces define a protocol for code communication.

- Use the `implements` keyword to create an interface.

- Mixins allow you to share code between classes.

- Extension methods allow you to give additional functionality to classes that are not your own.

Where to go from here?

To see how to use interfaces in the context of building a real app, check out the raywenderlich.com article State Management with Provider: https://www.raywenderlich.com/6373413-state-management-with-provider.

Once you learn how to use a hammer, everything will look like a nail. Now that you know about abstract classes and interfaces, you might be tempted to use them all the time. Don't over-engineer your apps, though. Start simple, and add abstraction as you need it.

Throughout this book, you've gotten a few ideas for writing clean code. However, the principles of building clean architecture take clean coding to a whole new level. You won't master the skill all at once, but reading books and articles and watching videos on the subject will help you grow as a software engineer.

Oh, one more thing.

```
Uif!tfdsfu!up!mfbsojoh!Ebsu!xfmm!jt!up!
dg"ewtkqwu"cpf"lwuv"vt{"vjkpiu0"Vlqfh#|rx*uh#uhdglqj#wklv/
#wkdw#reylrxvo|#ghvfulehv#|rx1#Kssh$nsf%
```

Chapter 10: Asynchronous Programming

By Jonathan Sande

You've come a long way in your study of the Dart programming language. This chapter is an important one, as it fills in the remaining gaps needed to complete your apprenticeship. In it, you'll not only learn how to deal with code that takes a long time to complete, but along the way, you'll also see how to handle errors, connect to a remote server and read data from a file.

Your computer does a lot of work, and it does the work so fast that you don't usually realize how much it's actually doing. Every now and then, though, especially on an older computer or phone, you may notice an app slow down or even freeze. This may express itself as **jank** during an animation: that annoying stutter that happens when the device is doing so much work that some animation frames get dropped.

Tasks that take a long time generally fall into two categories: I/O tasks, and computationally intensive tasks. I/O, or input-output, includes things like reading and writing files, accessing a database, or downloading content from the internet. These all happen outside the CPU, so the CPU has to wait for them to complete. Computationally intensive tasks, on the other hand, happen inside the CPU. These tasks may include things like decrypting data, performing a mathematical calculation, or parsing JSON.

As a developer, you have to think about how your app, and in particular your UI, will respond when it meets these time-consuming tasks. Can you imagine if a user clicked a download button in your app, and the app simply froze until the 20 MB download was complete? You'd be collecting one-star reviews in a hurry.

Thankfully, Dart has a powerful solution baked into the very core of the language that allows you to gracefully handle delays without blocking the responsiveness of your app.

Concurrency in Dart

A **thread** is a sequence of commands that a computer executes. Some programming languages support multithreading, which is running multiple threads at the same time, while others do not. Dart, in particular, is a single-threaded language.

"What? Was it designed back in 1990 or something?"

No, Dart was actually created in 2011, well into the age of multicore CPUs.

"What a waste of all those other processing cores!"

Ah, but no. This choice to be single-threaded was made very deliberately and has some great advantages as you'll soon see.

Parallelism vs. concurrency

To understand Dart's model for handling long-running tasks, and also to see why the creators of Dart decided to make Dart single-threaded, it's helpful to understand the difference between parallelism and concurrency. In common English, these words mean approximately the same thing, but in computer science, there's a distinction.

Parallelism is when multiple tasks run *at the same time* on multiple processors or CPU cores. **Concurrency**, on the other hand, is when multiple tasks take turns running on a single CPU core. When a restaurant has a single person alternately taking orders and clearing tables, that's concurrency. But a restaurant that has one person taking orders and a different person clearing tables, that's parallelism.

"It seems like parallelism is better."

It can be — when there's a lot of work to do and that work is easy to split into independent tasks. However, there are some disadvantages with parallelism, too.

A problem with parallelism

Little Susie has four pieces of chocolate left in the box next to her bed. She used to have ten, but she's already eaten six of them. She's saved the best ones for last, because after school today, three of her friends are coming home with her. She can't wait to share her chocolates with them. Imagine her horror, though, when she gets home and finds only two pieces of chocolate left in the box! After a lengthy investigation, it turns out that Susie's brother had discovered her stash and helped himself to two of the chocolates. From that day on, Susie always locked her box whenever she left home.

The same thing can happen in parallel threads that have access to the same memory. One thread saves a value in memory and expects the value to be the same when the thread checks the value later. However, if a second thread modifies the value, the first thread gets confused. It can be a major headache to track down those kinds of bugs because they come from a source completely separated from the code that reports the error. A language that supports multithreading needs to set up a system of locks so that values won't be changed at the wrong time. The cognitive load of designing, implementing, and debugging a system with multiple threads can be heavy, to say the least.

So the problem isn't so much with parallelism itself, but rather with multiple threads having access to the same state in memory.

Dart isolates

Dart's single thread runs in what it calls an **isolate**. Each isolate has its own allocated memory area, which ensures that no isolate can access any other isolate's state. That means that there's no need for a complicated locking system. It also means that sensitive data is much more secure. Such a system greatly reduces the cognitive load on a programmer.

But isn't concurrency slow?

If you're running all of a program's tasks on a single thread, it seems like it would be really slow. However, it turns out that that's not usually the case. In the following image, you can see tasks running on two threads in the top portion, and the same tasks running on a single thread in the bottom portion.

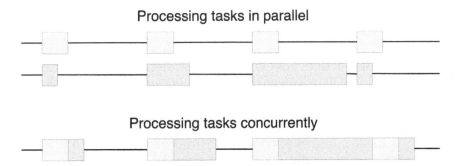

The concurrent version does take a little longer, but it isn't *much longer*. The reason is that the parallel threads were idle for much of the time. A single thread is usually more than enough to accomplish what needs to be done.

Flutter needs to update the UI 60 times a second, where each update timeslice is called a **frame**. That leaves about 16 milliseconds to redraw the UI on each frame. It doesn't take that long, normally, so that gives you additional time to perform other work while the thread is idle. As long as that work doesn't block Flutter from updating the UI on the next frame, the user won't notice any problems. The trick is to schedule tasks during the thread's downtimes.

Synchronous vs. asynchronous code

The word **synchronous** is composed of *syn*, meaning "together", and *chron*, meaning "time", thus *together in time*. Synchronous code is where each instruction is executed in order, one line of code immediately following the previous one.

This is in contrast to **asynchronous** code, which means *not* together in time. That is, with asynchronous code, certain tasks are rescheduled to be run in the future when the thread isn't busy.

All of the code that you've written so far in the book has been synchronous. For example:

```
print('first');
print('second');
print('third');
```

Run that and it prints:

```
first
second
third
```

Since the code is executed synchronously, it'll never print in a different order like third first second.

For many tasks, order matters. Multiplying before adding is different than adding before multiplying. You have to open the bottle before you can take a drink. For other tasks, though, the order doesn't matter. It doesn't matter if you brush your teeth first or wash your face first. It doesn't matter if you put a sock on the right foot first or the left foot first.

As in life, so it is with Dart. While some code needs to be executed in order, other tasks can be temporarily postponed. The postponable tasks are where the Dart event loop comes in.

The event loop

You've learned that Dart is based around concurrency on a single thread, but how does Dart manage to schedule tasks asynchronously? Dart uses what it calls an **event loop** to execute tasks that had previously been postponed.

The event loop has two queues: a **microtask queue** and an **event queue**. The microtask queue is mostly used internally by Dart. The event queue is for events like a user entering a keystroke or touching the screen, or data coming from a database, file, or remote server. Have a look at the following image:

- Synchronous tasks in the main isolate thread are always run immediately. You can't interrupt them.

- If Dart finds any long-running tasks that agree to be postponed, Dart puts them in the event queue.

- When Dart is finished running the synchronous tasks, the event loop checks the microtask queue. If the microtask queue has any tasks, the event loop puts them on the main thread to execute next. The event loop keeps checking the microtask queue until it's empty.

- If the synchronous tasks and microtask queue are both empty, then the event loop sends the next waiting task in the event queue to run in the main thread. Once it gets there, the code is executed synchronously. Just like any other synchronous code, nothing can interrupt it after it starts.

- If any new microtasks enter the microtask queue, the event loop always handles them before the next event in the event queue.

- This process continues until all of the queues are empty.

Running code in parallel

When people say Dart is single-threaded, they mean that Dart only runs on a single thread in the isolate. However, that *doesn't* mean you can't have tasks running on another thread. One example of this is when the underlying platform performs some work at the request of Dart. For example, when you ask to read a file on the system, that work isn't happening on the Dart thread. The system is doing the work inside its own process. Once the system finishes its work, it passes the result back to Dart, and Dart schedules some code to handle the result in the event queue. A lot of the I/O work from the dart:io library happens in this way.

Another way to perform work on other threads is to create a new Dart isolate. The new isolate has its own memory and its own thread working in parallel with the main isolate. The two isolates are only able to communicate through messages, though. They have no access to each other's memory state. The idea is similar to messaging a friend. Sending Ray a text message doesn't give you access to the internal memory of his mobile device. He simply checks his messages and replies to you when he feels like it.

You won't often need to create a new isolate. However, if you have a task that's taking too long on your main isolate thread, which you'll notice as unresponsiveness or jank in the UI, then this work is likely a good candidate for handing it off to another isolate. The final section of this chapter will tell you how to do that.

Futures

You now know, at a high level, how Dart handles asynchronous code with its event loop. Now it's time to learn how to work with asynchronous code at a practical level.

The Future type

Dart has a type called Future, which is basically a promise to give you the value you really want later. Here's the signature of a method that returns a future:

```
Future<int> countTheAtoms();
```

Future itself is generic; it can provide any type. In this case, though, the future is promising to give you an integer. In your code, if you called countTheAtoms, Dart would quickly return an object of type Future<int>. In effect, this is saying, "Hey, I'll get back to you with that int sometime later. Carry on!", in which case you'd proceed to run whatever synchronous code is next.

Behind the scenes, Dart has passed your request on to, presumably, an atom counting machine, which runs independently of your main Dart isolate. At this point, there is nothing on the event queue, and your main thread is free to do other things. Dart knows about the uncompleted future, though. When the atom counting machine finishes its work, it tells Dart and Dart puts the result, along with any code you gave it to handle the result, on the event queue. Dart says, "Sorry that took so long. Who knew that there were 9.2 quintillion atoms in that little grain of sand! I'll put your handling code at the end of the event queue. Give the event loop a few milliseconds and then it'll be your turn."

> **Note**: Since the largest an int can be on a 64 bit system is 9,223,372,036,854,775,807, or $2^{63} - 1$, it would be better to use BigInt as the return type of countTheAtoms. Although slower, BigInt can handle arbitrarily large numbers. When int values are too big at compile time, there's a compile-time error. However, at runtime, they overflow. That is, 9223372036854775807 + 1 == -9223372036854775808.

States for a future

Before a future completes, there isn't really anything you can do with it, but after it completes it will have two possible results: the value you were asking for, or an error. This all works out to three different states for a future:

- Uncompleted
- Completed with a value
- Completed with an error

Example of a future

One easy way to see a future in action is with the `Future.delayed` constructor.

```
final myFuture = Future<int>.delayed(
  Duration(seconds: 1),
  () => 42,
);
```

Here's what's happening:

- `myFuture` is of type `Future<int>`.

- The first argument is a `Duration`. After a delay of 1 second, Dart will add the anonymous function in the second argument to the event queue.

- When the event loop gets to `() => 42` it will run that function in the main isolate, which results in the function returning the integer 42.

In the future above, the value you really want is the 42, but how do you get it? Your variable `myFuture` isn't 42; it's a future that's a promise to return an `int` or an error. You can see that if you try to print `myFuture`:

```
print(myFuture);
```

The result is:

```
Instance of 'Future<int>'
```

There are two ways to get at the value after a future completes. One is with callbacks and the other is using the `async-await` syntax.

Getting the result with callbacks

A **callback** is an anonymous function that will run after some event has completed. In the case of a future, there are three callback opportunities: `then`, `catchError` and `whenComplete`.

Replace the body of the main function with the following code:

```
print('Before the future');

final myFuture = Future<int>.delayed(
  Duration(seconds: 1),
  () => 42,
)
```

```
    .then(
      (value) => print('Value: $value'),
    )
    .catchError(
      (error) => print('Error: $error'),
    )
    .whenComplete(
      () => print('Future is complete'),
    );

  print('After the future');
```

You recall that a future will either give you a value or an error. If it completes with a value, you can get the value by adding a callback to the then method. The anonymous function provides the value as an argument so that you have access to it. On the other hand, if the future completes with an error, you can handle it in catchError. Either way, though, whether the future completes with a value or an error, you have the opportunity to run any final code in whenComplete.

Run the code above to see these results:

```
Before the future
After the future
Value: 42
Future is complete.
```

Were you surprised that "After the future" was printed before the future results? That print statement is synchronous, so it ran immediately. Even if the future didn't have a one-second delay, it would still have to go to the event queue and wait for all the synchronous code to finish.

Getting the result with async-await

Callbacks are pretty easy to understand, but they can be hard to read, especially if you nest them in multiple layers. A more readable way to write the code above is using the async and await syntax. This syntax makes futures look much more like synchronous code.

Replace the entire main function with the following:

```
Future<void> main() async {
  print('Before the future');

  final value = await Future<int>.delayed(
    Duration(seconds: 1),
    () => 42,
```

```
  );
  print('Value: $value');

  print('After the future');
}
```

There are a few changes this time:

- If a function uses the `await` keyword, then it must return a `Future` and add the `async` keyword before the function body. Using `async` clearly tells Dart that this is an asynchronous function, and that the results will go to the event queue. Since `main` doesn't return a value, you use `Future<void>`.

- In front of the future, you added the `await` keyword. Once Dart sees `await`, the rest of the function won't run until the future completes. If the future completes with a value, there are no callbacks. You have direct access to that value. Thus, the type of the `value` variable above is not `Future`, but `int`.

Run the code above to see the following results:

```
Before the future
Value: 42
After the future
```

This time, "After the future" gets printed last. That's because *everything* after the `await` keyword is sent to the event queue.

What if the future returns an error, though?

For that, you need to learn about an error handling feature of Dart called a `try-catch` block.

Handling errors with try-catch blocks

The syntax of a `try-catch` block looks like this:

```
try {

} catch (error) {

} finally {

}
```

If you're attempting an operation that might result in an error, you'll place it in the try block. If there is an error, Dart will give you a chance to handle it in the catch block. And whether there is an error or not, you can run some last code in the finally block.

> **Note**: Dart has both an Exception type and an Error type. The words exception and error are often used interchangeably, but an Exception is something that you should expect and handle in the catch block. However, an Error is the result of a programming mistake. You should let the error crash your app as a sign that you need to fix whatever caused the error.

Try-catch blocks with async-await

Here's what the future looks like inside the try–catch block:

```
print('Before the future');

try {
  final value = await Future<int>.delayed(
    Duration(seconds: 1),
    () => 42,
  );
  print('Value: $value');
} catch (error) {
  print(error);
} finally {
  print('Future is complete');
}

print('After the future');
```

The catch and finally blocks correspond to the catchError and whenComplete callbacks that you saw earlier. If the future completes with an error, then the try block will immediately be aborted and the catch block will be called. But no matter whether the future completes with a value or an error, the finally block will always be called.

Run the code above to see the following result:

```
Before the future
Value: 42
Future is complete
After the future
```

The future finished with a value, so the catch block was not called.

Catching an error

In order to see what happens when there's an error, add the following line to the `try` block on the line immediately before `print('Value: $value')`:

```
throw Exception('There was an error');
```

The `throw` keyword is how you return an instance of `Exception` or `Error`.

Run the code again:

```
Before the future
Exception: There was an error
Future is complete
After the future
```

This time you can see that the `try` block never got a chance to print the value, but the `catch` block picked up the error message from the exception.

Asynchronous network requests

In the examples above, you used `Future.delayed` to simulate a task that takes a long time. Using `Future.delayed` is useful during app development for this same reason: You can implement an interface with a mock network request class to see how your UI will react while the app is waiting for a response.

As useful as `Future.delayed` is, though, eventually you'll need to implement the real network request class. The following example will show how to make an HTTP request to access a REST API. This example will make use of many of the concepts you've learned previously in this book.

> **Note**: HTTP, or **hypertext transfer protocol**, is a standard way of communicating with a remote server. REST, or **representational state transfer**, is an architectural style that includes commands like GET, POST, PUT, and DELETE. The API, or **application programing interface**, is similar in idea to the interfaces you made in Chapter 9. A remote server defines a specific API using REST commands which allow clients to access and modify resources on the server.

Creating a data class

The web API you're going to use will return some data about a todo list item. The data will be in JSON format, so in order to convert that into a more usable Dart object, you'll create a special class to hold the data.

Add the following code below the `main` function:

```
class Todo {
  Todo({
    required this.userId,
    required this.id,
    required this.title,
    required this.completed,
  });

  factory Todo.fromJson(Map<String, Object?> jsonMap) {
    return Todo(
      userId: jsonMap['userId'] as int,
      id: jsonMap['id'] as int,
      title: jsonMap['title'] as String,
      completed: jsonMap['completed'] as bool,
    );
  }

  final int userId;
  final int id;
  final String title;
  final bool completed;

  @override
  String toString() {
    return 'userId: $userId\n'
        'id: $id\n'
        'title: $title\n'
        'completed: $completed';
  }
}
```

This is all content that you learned in Chapter 6. You'll use the `fromJson` factory constructor in a minute.

Adding the necessary imports

The http package from the Dart team lets you make a GET request to a real server. Make sure your project has a **pubspec.yaml** file, and then add the following dependency:

```
dependencies:
  http: ^0.13.1
```

Save the file, and if necessary, run dart pub get in the terminal to pull the http package from Pub.

Then at the top of the file with your main function, add the following imports:

```
import 'dart:convert';
import 'dart:io';
import 'package:http/http.dart' as http;
```

Here's what each import is for:

- The dart:convert library will give you jsonDecode, a function for converting a raw JSON string to a Dart map.

- The dart:io library has HttpException and SocketException, which you'll use shortly.

- The final import is the http library that you just added to pubspec.yaml. Note the as http at the end. This isn't necessary, but the as keyword lets you prefix any functions from the library with the name http. You don't need to call it http — any arbitrary name is fine. Feel free to change the name to pinkElephants if you so desire. Providing a custom name can be useful for avoiding naming conflicts with other libraries or functions.

Making a GET request

Now that you have the necessary imports, replace your main function with the following code:

```
Future<void> main() async {
  final url = 'https://jsonplaceholder.typicode.com/todos/1';
  final parsedUrl = Uri.parse(url);
  final response = await http.get(parsedUrl);
  final statusCode = response.statusCode;
  if (statusCode == 200) {
    final rawJsonString = response.body;
    final jsonMap = jsonDecode(rawJsonString);
    final todo = Todo.fromJson(jsonMap);
```

```
    print(todo);
  } else {
    throw HttpException('$statusCode');
  }
}
```

There are a few new things here, so have a look at each of them:

- The URL address is for a server that provides an API that returns sample JSON for developers. It's very similar to the type of API you would make as a backend for a client app. `Uri.parse` converts the raw URL string to a format that `http.get` will recognize.

- You use `http.get` to make a GET request to the URL. Change `http` to `pinkElephants` if that's what you called it earlier. GET requests are the same kinds of requests that browsers make whenever you type a URL in the address bar.

- Since it takes time to contact a server that may exist in another continent, `http.get` returns a future. Dart passes off the work of contacting the remote server to the underlying platform, so you won't need to worry about it blocking your app while you wait. Since you are using the `await` keyword, the rest of the main method will be added to the event queue when the future completes. If the future completes with a value, the value will be an object of type `Response`, which includes information from the server.

- HTTP defines various three-digit status codes. A status code of `200` means `OK` — the request was successful and the server did what you asked of it. The common status code of `404`, on the other hand, means the server couldn't find what you were asking for. If that happens you'll throw an `HttpException`.

- The response body from this URL address includes a string in JSON format. You use `jsonDecode` from the `dart:convert` library to convert the raw JSON string into a Dart map.

- Once you have a Dart `map`, you can pass it into the `fromJson` factory constructor of your `Todo` class that you wrote earlier.

Make sure you have an internet connection, then run the code above. You'll see a printout from your `Todo` object's `toString` method:

```
userId: 1
id: 1
title: delectus aut autem
completed: false
```

The values of each field come from the remote server.

Handling errors

There are a few things that could go wrong with the code above, so you'll need to be ready to handle any errors that come up. First, surround all the code inside the body of the `main` function with a `try` block:

```
try {
  final url = 'https://jsonplaceholder.typicode.com/todos/1';
  // ...
}
```

Then below the `try` block, add the following `catch` blocks:

```
on SocketException catch (error) {
  print(error);
} on HttpException catch (error) {
  print(error);
} on FormatException catch (error) {
  print(error);
}
```

These `catch` blocks handle specific types of errors. You use the on keyword to specify the name of the exception. Here's what each one means:

- **SocketException**: You'll get this exception if there's no internet connection. The `http.get` method is the one to throw the exception.

- **HttpException**: You're throwing this exception yourself if the status code is not `200 OK`.

- **FormatException**: `jsonDecode` throws this exception if the JSON string from the server isn't in proper JSON format. It would be unwise to blindly trust whatever the server gives you.

> **Note:** It's good to be specific in your error catching. That way if a different kind of error comes up that you weren't expecting, your app will fail with a crash. That might sound bad, but it means you can fix the error right away instead of silently ignoring it as a generic `catch` block would do.

Testing a socket exception

Turn off your internet and run the code again. You should see the following output:

```
SocketException: Failed host lookup:
'jsonplaceholder.typicode.com'
```

In an actual app, instead of just printing a message to the console, you'd probably want to remind the user to turn on their internet.

Turn *your* internet back on and proceed to the next test.

Testing an HTTP exception

Change the URL to the following:

```
final url = 'https://jsonplaceholder.typicode.com/todos/pink-
elephants';
```

Unless https://jsonplaceholder.typicode.com has recently added the /pink-elephants URL endpoint, you should get a 404 when you run the code again:

```
HttpException: 404
```

In a real app, you'd inform the user that whatever they were looking for isn't available.

Restore the URL as it was before:

```
final url = 'https://jsonplaceholder.typicode.com/todos/1';
```

Testing a JSON format exception

Replace the following line:

```
final rawJsonString = response.body;
```

with this:

```
final rawJsonString = 'abc';
```

Since abc isn't properly formatted JSON, you'll see the following error when you run the code again:

```
FormatException: Unexpected character (at character 1)
abc
^
```

Nice work! You now know how to get the value from a future and handle any errors.

After you finish the following mini-exercises, you'll learn about streams, a concept closely related to futures.

Mini-exercises

1. Use the `Future.delayed` constructor to provide a string after two seconds that says "I am from the future."

2. Create a `String` variable named `message` that awaits the future to complete with a value.

3. Surround the code above with a `try-catch` block.

Streams

A future represents a single value that will arrive in the future. A **stream**, on the other hand, represents *multiple* values that will arrive in the future. Think of a stream like a list of futures. You can imagine a stream meandering through the woods as the autumn leaves fall onto the surface of the water. Each time a leaf floats by, it's like the value that a Dart stream provides.

Streaming music online as opposed to downloading the song before playing it is another good comparison. When you stream music, you get lots of little chunks of data, but when you download the whole file, you only get a single value, which is the entire file — a little like what a future returns. In fact, the `http.get` command you used in the last section was actually implemented as a stream internally. However, Dart just waited until the stream finished and then returned all of the data at once in the form of a completed future.

Streams, which are of type `Stream`, are used extensively in Dart and Dart-based frameworks. Here are some examples:

- Reading a large file stored locally where new data from the file comes in chunks.

- Downloading a file from a remote server.

- Listening for requests coming into a server.

- Representing user events such as button clicks.

- Relaying changes in app state to the UI.

While it's possible to build your own streams from scratch, most of the time you don't need to do that. You only need to be able to use the streams that Dart or a Dart package provides for you, which is what this section will teach you.

Subscribing to a stream

The dart:io library contains a File class which allows you to read data from a file. First, you'll read data the easy way using the readAsString method, which returns the contents of the file as a future. Then you'll do it again by reading the data as a stream of bytes.

Adding an assets file

You need a text file to work with, so you'll add that to your project now.

Create a new folder named **assets** in the root of your project. In that folder, create a file named **text.txt**. Add some text to the file. Although any text will work, *Lorem Ipsum* is a good standby:

```
Lorem ipsum dolor sit amet, consectetur adipiscing elit, sed do
eiusmod tempor incididunt ut labore et dolore magna aliqua. Ut
enim ad minim veniam, quis nostrud exercitation ullamco laboris
nisi ut aliquip ex ea commodo consequat. Duis aute irure dolor
in reprehenderit in voluptate velit esse cillum dolore eu fugiat
nulla pariatur. Excepteur sint occaecat cupidatat non proident,
sunt in culpa qui officia deserunt mollit anim id est laborum.
```

Then save the file.

> **Note:** *Lorem Ipsum* is often used as filler text by graphic designers and app developers when the meaning of the text doesn't matter. The Latin words were taken from the writings of the Roman statesman and philosopher Cicero but modified so as to become essentially meaningless.

Reading as a string

Now that you've created the text file, replace your Dart code with the following:

```dart
import 'dart:io';

Future<void> main() async {
  final file = File('assets/text.txt');
  final contents = await file.readAsString();
  print(contents);
}
```

Here's what's new:

- `File` takes the relative path to your text file as the argument.

- `readAsString` returns `Future<String>`, but by using `await` you'll receive the string itself when it's ready.

`File` also has a `readAsStringSync` method, which would run synchronously and avoid awaiting a future. However, doing so would block your app if the reading takes a while. Many of the methods on `File` have synchronous versions, but in order to prevent blocking your app, you should generally prefer the asynchronous versions.

Run the code above, and you'll see the contents of `text.txt` printed to the console.

Increasing the file size

If the file is large, you can read it as a stream. This allows you to start processing the data more quickly, since you don't have to wait to finish reading the entire file as you did in the last example.

When you read a file as a stream, it reads the file in chunks. The size of the chunks depends on how Dart is implemented on the system you're using, but it's probably 65,536 bytes per chunk as it was on the local machines used when writing this chapter. The `text.txt` file with *Lorem Ipsum* that you created earlier is only 445 bytes, so that means trying to stream that file would be no different than simply reading the whole thing as you did before.

In order to get a text file large enough to stream in chunks, create a new file in the **assets** folder called **text_long.txt**. Copy the *Lorem Ipsum* text and paste it in **text_long.txt** as new lines so that there are 1000 *Lorem Ipsum* copies. You can of course select-all and recopy from time to time, unless you find it therapeutic to paste things a thousand times. Save the file and you'll be ready to proceed.

Alternatively, you can find **text_long.txt** in the **assets** folder of the **final** project that comes with this chapter.

Reading from a stream

Replace the contents in the body of the `main` function with the following code:

```
final file = File('assets/text_long.txt');
final stream = file.openRead();
stream.listen(
  (data) {
    print(data.length);
```

```
    },
);
```

Here are a few points to note:

- Instead of calling readAsString on file, this time you're calling openRead, which returns an object of type Stream<List<int>>. That's a lot of angle brackets, but Stream<List<int>> simply means that it's a stream that periodically produces a list, and that list is a list of integers. The integers are the byte values, and the list is the chunk of data that's being passed in.

- To subscribe for notifications whenever there's new data coming in the stream, you call the listen method and pass it an anonymous function that takes a single parameter. The data parameter here is of type List<int>, so now you have access to the chunk of data coming in from the file.

- Since each integer in the list is one byte, calling data.length will tell you the number of bytes in the chunk.

> **Note**: By default, only a single object can listen to a stream. This is known as a **single subscription stream**. If you want more than one object to be notified of stream events, you need to create a **broadcast stream**, which you could do like so:
>
> ```
> final broadcastStream = stream.asBroadcastStream();
> ```

Run the code in main and you should see something similar to the following:

```
65536
65536
65536
65536
65536
65536
52783
```

The data, at least on the computer used while writing this chapter, was all in 65,536-byte chunks until the final one, which was smaller since it didn't quite fill up the 65,536-byte buffer size. Your final chunk may be a different size than the one shown here, depending on how therapeutic your copy-and-paste session was.

Using an asynchronous for loop

Just as you can use callbacks or `async-await` to get the value of a future, there are also two ways to get the values of a stream. In the example above, you used the `listen` callback. Here is the same example using an asynchronous `for` loop:

```
Future<void> main() async {
  final file = File('assets/text_long.txt');
  final stream = file.openRead();
  await for (var data in stream) {
    print(data.length);
  }
}
```

The `await for` keywords cause the loop to pause until the next data event comes in. Run this and you'll see the same results as before.

Error handling

Like futures, stream events can also produce an error rather than a value. You can handle errors using a callback or `try-catch` blocks.

Using a callback

One way to handle errors is to use the `onError` callback like so:

```
final file = File('assets/text_long.txt');
final stream = file.openRead();
stream.listen(
  (data) {
    print(data.length);
  },
  onError: (error) {
    print(error);
  },
  onDone: () {
    print('All finished');
  },
);
```

Here are a couple of points to note:

- When an error occurs, it won't cancel the stream, and you'll continue to receive more data events. If you actually did want to cancel the stream after an error, then `listen` also has a `cancelOnError` parameter which you can set to `true`.

- When a stream finishes sending all of its data, it'll fire a done event. This gives you a chance to respond with an onDone callback.

Using try-catch

The other way to handle errors on a stream is with a try-catch block in combination with async-await. Here is what that looks like:

```
try {
  final file = File('assets/text_long.txt');
  final stream = file.openRead();
  await for (var data in stream) {
    print(data.length);
  }
} on Exception catch (error) {
    print(error);
} finally {
  print('All finished');
}
```

In this example, you're catching all exceptions. A more robust solution would check for specific errors like FileSystemException, which would be thrown if the file didn't exist.

Run either the callback version, or the try-catch version, and you'll see the same chunk sizes as before, with the additional text "All finished" printed at the end.

Change the filename to something nonexistent, like pink_elephants.txt, and run the code again. Confirm that you have a FileSystemException.

```
FileSystemException: Cannot open file, path = 'assets/
pink_elephants.txt' (OS Error: No such file or directory, errno
= 2)
All finished
```

Even with the exception, the finally block, or onDone callback if that's what you used, still printed "All finished".

Cancelling a stream

As mentioned above, you may use the cancelOnError parameter to tell the stream that you want to stop listening in the event of an error. However, even if there isn't an error, you should always cancel your subscription to a stream if you no longer need it. This allows Dart to clean up the memory the stream was using. Failing to do so can cause a memory leak.

Replace your Dart code with the following version:

```
import 'dart:async';
import 'dart:io';

Future<void> main() async {
  final file = File('assets/text_long.txt');
  final stream = file.openRead();
  StreamSubscription<List<int>>? subscription;
  subscription = stream.listen(
    (data) {
      print(data.length);
      subscription?.cancel();
    },
    cancelOnError: true,
    onDone: () {
      print('All finished');
    },
  );
}
```

Calling `listen` returns a `StreamSubscription`, which is part of the `dart:async` library. Keeping a reference to that in the `subscription` variable allows you to cancel the subscription whenever you want. In this case, you cancel it after the first data event.

Run the code and you'll only see 65536 printed once. The `onDone` callback was never called because the stream never completed.

Transforming a stream

Being able to transform a stream as the data is coming in is very powerful. In the examples above, you never did anything with the data except print the length of the list of bytes. Those bytes represent text, though, so you're going to transform the data from numbers to text.

For this demonstration, there's no need to use a large text file so you'll switch back to the 445-byte version of *Lorem Ipsum* in **text.txt**.

Viewing the bytes

Replace the contents of `main` with the following code:

```
final file = File('assets/text.txt');
final stream = file.openRead();
stream.listen(
  (data) {
```

```
    print(data);
  },
);
```

Run that and you'll see a long list of bytes in decimal form:

```
[76, 111, 114, 101, ... ]
```

Although different computers encode text files using different encodings, the abbreviated list above is from a computer that uses UTF-8 encoding. You may recall that UTF-16 uses 16-bit, or 2-byte, code units to encode Unicode text. UTF-8 uses one to four 8-bit units to encode Unicode text. Since for values of 127 and below, UTF-8 and Unicode code points are the same, English text only takes one byte per letter. This makes file sizes smaller than UTF-16 encoding, which is beneficial when saving to disk or sending over a network.

If you look up 76 in Unicode you'll see that it's the capital letter **L**, 111 is **o**, and on it goes with `Lorem ipsum dolor sit`....

Decoding the bytes

Next, you'll take the UTF-8 bytes and convert them to a string.

Make sure you have the following imports and `main` method:

```
import 'dart:convert';
import 'dart:io';

Future<void> main() async {
  final file = File('assets/text.txt');
  final stream = file.openRead();
  await for (var data in stream.transform(utf8.decoder)) {
    print(data);
  }
}
```

The difference here is that you added the `transform` method to the stream. This method takes the input from the original stream, transforms it with a `StreamTransformer`, and outputs a new stream, which you can listen to or loop over as before. In this case, the stream transformer was the `dart:convert` library's `utf8.decoder`, which takes a list of bytes and converts them to a string.

Run the code and you'll see the *Lorem Ipsum* passage printed in plain text.

Mini-exercises

The following code produces a stream that outputs an integer every second and then stops after the tenth time.

```
Stream<int>.periodic(
  Duration(seconds: 1),
  (value) => value,
).take(10);
```

1. Set the stream above to a variable named myStream.

2. Use await for to print the value of the integer on each data event coming from the stream.

Isolates

Most of the time it's fine to run your own code synchronously, and for long-running I/O tasks, you can use Dart libraries that return futures or streams. However you may sometimes discover that your code is too computationally expensive and degrades the performance of your app.

App stopping synchronous code

Have a look at this example:

```
String playHideAndSeekTheLongVersion() {
  var counting = 0;
  for (var i = 1; i <= 10000000000; i++) {
    counting = i;
  }
  return '$counting! Ready or not, here I come!';
}
```

Counting to ten billion takes a while — even for a computer! If you run that function in a Flutter app, your app's UI would freeze until the function finishes.

Try running that function from main like so:

```
print("OK, I'm counting...");
print(playHideAndSeekTheLongVersion());
```

You'll notice a significant wait until the counting finishes.

App stopping asynchronous code

Since you've read this far in the chapter, you should be aware that making the function asynchronous doesn't fix the problem:

```
Future<String> playHideAndSeekTheLongVersion() async {
  var counting = 0;
  await Future(() {
    for (var i = 1; i <= 10000000000; i++) {
      counting = i;
    }
  });
  return '$counting! Ready or not, here I come!';
}
```

Run that using `await`:

```
print("OK, I'm counting...");
print(await playHideAndSeekTheLongVersion());
```

Adding the computationally intensive loop as an anonymous function in a `Future` constructor does indeed make it a future. However, think about what's going on here. Dart simply puts that anonymous function at the end of the event queue. True, all the events before it will get to go first, but once the 10-billion-counter-loop gets to the end of the queue, it'll start running synchronously and block the app until it finishes. Using a future only delays the eventual block.

Spawning an isolate

When you're used to using futures from the Dart I/O libraries, it's easy to get lulled into thinking that futures always run in the background, but that's not the case. If you want to run some computationally intensive code on another thread, then you'll need to create a new isolate to do that.

The term for creating an isolate in Dart is called **spawning**. Since isolates don't share any memory with each other, they can only communicate by sending messages. When you spawn a new isolate, you give it a message communication object called a **send port**. The new isolate uses the send port to send messages back to a **receive port**, which is listening on the main isolate.

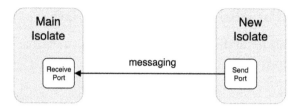

In this example, the communication is only one way, although it's also possible to set up two-way communication between isolates.

Using a send port to return results

Add the new version of playHideAndSeekTheLongVersion as a top level method in your file:

```
import 'dart:isolate';

void playHideAndSeekTheLongVersion(SendPort sendPort) {
  var counting = 0;
  for (var i = 1; i <= 1000000000; i++) {
    counting = i;
  }
  sendPort.send('$counting! Ready or not, here I come!');
}
```

Note that now it's a void function that takes a SendPort object as a parameter. SendPort is like one of those emergency mobile phones for kids where the phone can only call home. Home in this case is the main isolate. Instead of returning a string from the function like you were doing before, this time you're sending it as a message over the send port. Back in the main isolate, there will be a receive port listening for the message.

Spawning the isolate and listening for messages

Replace the main method with the following code:

```
Future<void> main() async {
  // 1
  final receivePort = ReceivePort();

  // 2
  final isolate = await Isolate.spawn(
    playHideAndSeekTheLongVersion,
    // 3
    receivePort.sendPort,
  );
```

```
  // 4
  receivePort.listen((message) {
    print(message);
    // 5
    receivePort.close();
    isolate.kill();
  });
}
```

Here's what you did:

1. You created a receive port to listen for messages from the new isolate.

2. Next, you spawned a new isolate and gave it two arguments. The first argument is the function that you want the isolate to execute. That function must be a top-level or static function. It must also take a single parameter. The second argument of spawn will be passed as the argument to playHideAndSeekTheLongVersion.

3. The receivePort has a sendPort that belongs to it. This is the part where Mommy gives little Timmy the phone and says to call home if anything happens. The second parameter of spawn isn't actually required to be a SendPort object, but how is Timmy going to call home without a phone? If you want to pass additional parameters to the function, you can make the second parameter of spawn be a list or a map in which one of the elements is a SendPort and the other elements are additional arguments.

4. Finally, receivePort.listen gets a callback whenever sendPort sends a message. This is where Mommy carries her phone with her wherever she goes, always waiting for a call from Timmy.

5. In this example, the isolate is no longer needed after the work is done, so you can close the receive port and kill the isolate to free up the memory. This is where the Mommy-Timmy analogy fails. Mommy goes and saves Timmy before anything bad happens.

Note: The Flutter framework has a highly simplified way to start a new isolate, perform some work, and then return the result using a function called compute. Rather than passing the function a send port, you just pass it any values that are needed. In this case, you could just pass it the number to count to:

```
await compute(playHideAndSeekTheLongVersion, 10000000000);
```

That's enough to get you started on working with isolates. As a word of advice, though, don't feel like you need to preoptimize everything you think might be a computationally intensive task. Write your code as if it will all run on the main isolate. Only after you encounter performance problems will you need to start thinking about moving some code to a separate isolate.

Challenges

Before moving on, here are some challenges to test your knowledge of asynchronous programming. It's best if you try to solve them yourself, but if you get stuck, solutions are available in the **challenge** folder of this chapter.

Challenge 1: Whose turn is it?

This is a fun one and will test how well you understand how Dart handles asynchronous tasks. In what order will Dart print the text with the following `print` statements? Why?

```
void main() {
  print('1 synchronous');
  Future(() => print('2 event queue')).then(
    (value) => print('3 synchronous'),
  );
  Future.microtask(() => print('4 microtask queue'));
  Future.microtask(() => print('5 microtask queue'));
  Future.delayed(
    Duration(seconds: 1),
    () => print('6 event queue'),
  );
  Future(() => print('7 event queue')).then(
    (value) => Future(() => print('8 event queue')),
  );
  Future(() => print('9 event queue')).then(
    (value) => Future.microtask(
      () => print('10 microtask queue'),
    ),
  );
  print('11 synchronous');
}
```

Try to answer before checking. If you're right, give yourself a well-deserved pat on the back!

Challenge 2: Care to make a comment?

The following link returns a JSON list of comments:

```
https://jsonplaceholder.typicode.com/comments
```

Create a `Comment` data class and convert the raw JSON to a Dart list of type `List<Comment>`.

Challenge 3: Data stream

The following code allows you to stream content from the given URL:

```
final url = Uri.parse('https://raywenderlich.com');
final client = http.Client();
final request = http.Request('GET', url);
final response = await client.send(request);
final stream = response.stream;
```

Your challenge is to transform the stream from bytes to strings and see how many bytes each data chunk is. Add error handling, and when the stream is finished, close the client.

Challenge 4: Fibonacci from afar

In Challenge 4 of Chapter 4, you wrote some code to calculate the nth Fibonacci number. Repeat that challenge, but run the code in a separate isolate. Pass the value of n to the new isolate as an argument, and send the result back to the main isolate.

Key points

- Dart is single-threaded and handles asynchronous programming through concurrency, rather than through parallelism.

- Concurrency refers to rescheduling tasks to run later on the same thread, while parallelism refers to running tasks at the same time on different threads.

- The way Dart implements the scheduling of asynchronous tasks is by using an event loop, which has an event queue and a microtask queue.

- Synchronous code always runs first and cannot be interrupted. This is followed by anything in the microtask queue, and when these are completed, by any tasks in the event queue.

- You may run Dart code on another thread only by spawning a new isolate.

- Dart isolates do not share any memory state and may only communicate through messages.

- Using a future, which is of type `Future`, tells Dart that the requested task may be rescheduled on the event loop.

- When a future completes, it will contain either the requested value or an error.

- A method that returns a future doesn't necessarily run on a different process or thread. That depends entirely on the implementation.

- A stream, which is of type `Stream`, is a series of futures.

- Using a stream enables you to handle data events as they happen rather than waiting for them all to finish.

- You can handle errors on futures and streams with callbacks or `try-catch` blocks.

Where to go from here?

This chapter taught you how to use futures and streams, but a good next step would be learning how to create them yourself. There's also a lot more that you can do through stream manipulation.

If you enjoyed making HTTP requests to access resources from a remote server, you should consider server-side development with Dart as well. Being able to use a single language for both the frontend and the backend is nothing short of amazing. No cognitive switching is required, because everything you learned in this book applies to writing Dart code on the server.

Conclusion

Congratulations! You've reached the end of *Dart Apprentice*. We hope you've enjoyed reading this book and that the skills you've acquired will help you in all your future Dart projects.

You're now fully prepared for success with Dart development in Flutter mobile, Flutter desktop, servers, websites or even command-line apps. There is, of course, much more to learn, but most of that learning will just be diving deeper into topics that you've already studied.

Thank you for deciding to learn Dart and thank you even more to do so by reading this book.

If you have any questions or comments, please stop by our forums at forums.raywenderlich.com and look for the particular forum category for this book.

Thank you again for purchasing this book. Your continued support is what makes the books, tutorials, videos and other things we do at raywenderlich.com possible. We truly appreciate it!

– The *Dart Apprentice* team

CPSIA information can be obtained
at www.ICGtesting.com
Printed in the USA
LVHW111521040122
707835LV00006B/387

9 781950 325320